THE BOMB AND YOUNG PEOPLE

Other titles in this series:

AIDS and Young People by Patrick Dixon
Drugs and Young People by Grahame Knox
Sex and Young People by Lance Pierson
The Occult and Young People by Roger Ellis

The Bomb
and
Young People

PETE GILBERT

KINGSWAY PUBLICATIONS
EASTBOURNE

Biblical quotations are from the
New International Version (NIV) © International Bible
Society 1973, 1978, 1984.

Front cover photo: The Photo Source

British Library Cataloguing in Publication Data

Gilbert, Pete
   The bomb and young people.
   1. Nuclear warfare—Christian viewpoints
   I. Title
   261.8'73

ISBN 0-86065-552-0

Printed in Great Britain for
KINGSWAY PUBLICATIONS LTD
1 St Anne's Road, Eastbourne, E Sussex BN21 3UN by
Richard Clay Ltd, Bungay, Suffolk
Typeset by Nuprint Ltd, Harpenden, Herts AL5 4SE.

Dedication

This book is dedicated with my love and thanks to my wife Nikki, whose unfailing love and patience for me has shown me the peace of God in action.

My thanks go to the two main bodies where my vision for God's kingdom is worked out: Revelation Christian Fellowship, (Bognor Regis and Chichester), and the Pioneer Team. I am proud to be a part of them both.

Contents

Preface

This book has been a long time in the writing. Not because I'm not passionately concerned with the subject. I am. I hate war and violence; I love young people. But rather because times change, and in the world of warfare, they change very quickly. I've tried to show this in the book. Even as this book was in the final stages of production, the politicians were rewriting the history books as the Cold War went through what appeared to be its final thaw. But while the politicians come and go, the Bomb remains.

This book is the result of a lot of hard praying, thinking, reading and talking. It's my hope that it's going to challenge you, annoy you, provoke you, sadden you and, most of all, help you see that only in the Prince of peace, in Jesus, can there be real peace. Times may change, but Jesus Christ doesn't. And if you're not a Christian, you need to hear this. There is hope. Read on and find out.

I

Nothing New under the Sun

This is a book about the Bomb. Not just *a* bomb, but *the* Bomb. Because of the steady and almost inexorable march of history, the events that occurred in 1945, though removed from us now by more than forty years, have not only shaped the years that span the Second World War and today, but have continued to dominate the history of the world. And one day they may determine the end of that history.

This book is an attempt to make a discussion of a complex subject not only understandable, but readable. I am not by any stretch of the imagination a scientifically minded person, so I figure that if I can grasp the facts behind the Bomb, then so can you. Scientific I am not, but passionately concerned I am. It may be that as you read about the arguments for and against nuclear warfare, you too will become passionate in your convictions, if you're not already.

But before we all disappear under a welter of personal opinion and emotions, I want to draw back and take a more objective historical view of the whole thing. The arguments come later in the book. For now, what am I writing about? What are nuclear bombs, and how did we first get them? Why were they first used, and what's happened since?

History is bunk

So said Henry Ford, father of the modern motor car. Yet history is the backcloth against which all the current themes of nuclear defence, deterrent and development take place. It's very hard nowadays to imagine a pre-nuclear world, even though the nuclear age was birthed less than half a century ago. I sometimes only realise the threat we live under when I try to imagine a world without the capacity to annihilate itself in one go. A world without nuclear arsenals, nuclear waste and pollution, and nuclear accidents would be very different. Politics would be very different. Threat levels of total annihilation would be greatly reduced. Suddenly it feels like a load has left your shoulders. That load— the threat and insanity of nuclear warfare—has been placed there by history. Let's make no mistakes: history is *not* bunk! If we don't learn from our past mistakes, if we don't understand where we've come from, we may not only fail to realise where we're heading, but much worse, we may never even get there! We *must* let history give us perspective, or else we make the old adage dangerously true: 'History repeats itself...it has to, no one listens!'

What is the Bomb?

Nuclear energy is based on an understanding of the properties of the basic 'building blocks' that make up our observable universe. Atoms are the basic blocks of which all matter is comprised. Each atom has a nucleus or central cluster of both neutrons and protons (positively charged). This cluster is in turn surrounded by electrons (negatively charged). When the nuclei or centres of certain atoms (heavy atoms, such as uranium) are struck by another neutron, then those atoms will split in two. This is known as nuclear fission. Fusion occurs when the atoms' nuclei combine (or fuse) rather than split. Now, when a neutron hits an atom's nucleus (a group of neutrons and protons) in this way, between one and three 'spare' neutrons are released. These 'spare' neutrons can in turn be used to bombard other atoms' nuclei creating further fission. This is called a chain reaction, or the 'K factor'. When this chain reaction is controlled (by deciding how many 'spare' neutrons go on colliding with atoms' nuclei and at what speed) you produce a controlled chain reaction in a nuclear reactor providing energy. A by-product of this process is a new, highly fissionable material called plutonium. When the chain reaction is *not* controlled and the speed of the reaction is very sudden, a nuclear explosion is produced. And when that explosion is deliberate and directive, you have in other words produced the Bomb.

The original nuclear bombs tended to be 'A' bombs ('A' for atom or atomic). They were fission bombs using plutonium or uranium for their 'heavy' atoms. The subsequent generation of nuclear bombs were 'H' bombs perfected in 1945, where 'H' stands for hydrogen which in the explosion converts to helium. These H bombs, detonated by a mini A bomb to produce the high temperatures needed to fuse two 'heavy' atomic materials, are about four times more powerful than A bombs. Both A and H bombs are currently held in the world's nuclear arsenals.

Birth pangs

The conception of such weapons of destruction can be traced all the way back to 1895 with the discovery by French scientist, Henry Becquerel of radioactivity. Its value was subsequently determined in medicine (x-rays) by pioneers like Marie Curie. But it wasn't seen as a potential source of energy (at first you had to put more in than you ever got back out) until much later than Becquerel.

By December 1938 a German scientist named Hahn had proposed and was testing the theory of nuclear fission. It was a short step from here to the possible use of nuclear power in some kind of Superbomb, though the technical difficulties to be overcome were awesome. These included obtaining enough fissionable material, whether or not there would be a nuclear 'bang' or a nuclear 'pop', and whether any bomb would be both too expensive and too heavy to deliver against an enemy.

Nonetheless, once you realise the potential of nuclear power, you realise its potential as a bomb. It was a fearsome thought to the British that immediately before the Second World War, Germany was on the threshold of such power. Consequently, it was the British scientists who began to lead the field in nuclear theory in the late 1930s and early 1940s. It had not gone unnoticed that as early as 1939, on the brink of the war, that Germany had stopped the sale of uranium from Czechoslovakian mines. The race was on!

Meanwhile, fleeing from Hitler's Nazi oppression across Europe, many of the leading physicists had reached the United States of America. Here, in co-operation with the British government, experimentation went on at a feverish pace to develop a Superbomb. As British resources were sapped by the war in Europe, the USA came to dominate the research scene. Albert Einstein had already written to President Roosevelt on 2nd August 1939, clearly forecasting the possibility of such a weapon.

> It may become possible to set up a nuclear chain reaction...by which vast amounts of power and large quantities of new radium-like elements would be generated...this...would also lead to the construction of bombs...extremely powerful bombs of a new type may thus be constructed. A single bomb of this type, carried by boat and exploded in a port, might very well destroy the whole port together with some of the surrounding territory. However, such bombs might very well prove to be too heavy for transportation by air.

President Roosevelt was determined to develop this new Superbomb. Julius Oppenheimer, a nuclear physicist, headed up Roosevelt's programme to research the nuclear bomb, and a host of top scientific minds joined him, including Niels Bohr, Enrico Fermi, Leo Szilard and Albert Einstein.

Blueprints

But the first blueprint for *the* Bomb had been drafted in the British Isles on 19th March 1940 by two European physicists, Frisch and Peierls. Their theoretical work led to the British government setting up the Maud Committee to investigate the claims these two scientists were making for their proposed Superbomb. They had claimed that

> the energy liberated in the explosion of such a Superbomb is about the same as that produced by the explosion of 1,000 tonnes of dynamite. This energy is liberated in a

small volume, in which it will, for an instant, produce a temperature comparable to that in the interior of the sun. The blast from such an explosion would destroy life in a wide area. The size of this area is difficult to estimate, but it will probably cover the centre of a big city.

By July 1941 the Maud Committee had reached its own conclusion, and these conclusions brought the development of nuclear bombs that much closer. For the Maud report indicated that far less active material was needed to make a viable weapon. Suddenly the bomb came within reach. At last both military and scientific minds could grasp the concept—it was not only desirable, but feasible.

We have now reached the conclusion that it will be possible to make an effective uranium bomb which, containing some 25 pounds of active material, would be equivalent as regards destructive effects to 1,800 tonnes of TNT and will also release large quantities of radioactive substances, which would make places near to where the bomb exploded dangerous to human life for a long period.

But to a large extent the Maud Committee and the British government had to back out of the developing nuclear race as the country worked to the very edge of its capacity in the war effort. And now the USA took over in what has been the most remarkable, concerted, speedy scientific and technological revolution *of all time*, fired as it necessarily was by the impetus of war. The development of the nuclear arms race has made the speed of the technology of the Space Race look like a snail's pace!

For on 7th December 1941, Japan had bombed Pearl Harbour and wholeheartedly, though belatedly, the USA now joined the Second World War. And so it was that in the throes of a worldwide conflict was born the final countdown to the development of *the* Bomb. President Roosevelt put a *massive* research programme into motion called the Manhattan Project. With full co-operation from the British government this project, drawing as it did on the greatest brains in physics, was to crack the feasibility and technical problems surrounding the production of the world's first nuclear bombs.

By December 1942 Enrico Fermi and his team undertook critical experiments in the squash court at Chicago University (!) and finally succeeded in obtaining the world's first sustained nuclear reactor. In those days the reactor was called a 'pile', and pile it was—of graphite blocks interspersed with uranium blocks. Placed strategically through these two kinds of blocks were cadmium control rods. These rods absorb the 'spare' neutrons released as the graphite and uranium react together. As the rods were progressively removed, so the pile moved towards the critical, until finally the readings indicated that the spare neutrons were now spontaneously reacting with a steady output of energy—in other words, the nuclear 'fire' had been safely lit, and a controlled nuclear chain reaction was taking place for the first time in history. And now the by-product of plutonium was available in quantities and purities sufficient to experiment viably with a bomb.

Nonetheless, it took a further two and a half years to develop that bomb. Plans had been in preparation in the USA to produce fissionable material, and everyone now believed it was only a matter of time. Who would win the race?

The race won

The answer came via the Manhattan project, for on 16th July 1945, twenty miles from the nearest town, Alamogordo, the world's first nuclear bomb was tested. Those scientists who had worked so hard for this day all gathered to see the results of their labours. There was still plenty of doubt as to what would happen; would it be a nuclear 'bang' or a 'pop'? Fermi was taking bets that the bomb might set fire to the earth's atmosphere and so destroy the whole planet. (Prophetic, this?!) The bomb, a plutonium weapon, was placed at the top of a steel tower and then armed. All around the tower at various distances were recording instruments, and further away by some twenty miles, the scientific and military observers. At 5.30 am on Monday 16th July 1945, the bomb was exploded, with an estimated force of 20,000 tonnes of TNT. Twenty-two miles away the hills lit up as though by a mid-day sun. The centre of the explosion itself was brighter than our sun, the noise and blast indescribable. For the first time in human history, the now all-too-familiar 'mushroom' cloud erupted upwards 40,000 feet from the earth's surface like an ugly excrescence warning of an impending disease. *The* Bomb was a success. The world had gone nuclear.

Use the Bomb!

What the ingenuity (or depravity) of man can devise, sooner or later the pride of man will make. And what man makes, sooner or later, the foolishness of man will test and use. And so it was that only three weeks after the first nuclear bomb test, the bomb was used against a city.

It's hard to understand why the bomb 'had' to be

used. Indeed, on hindsight the decision to drop the bomb on Japan can be seen as a political rather than a military one. From a military point of view the bomb didn't have to be used at all. The USA was already winning the war against Japan (particularly with saturation air-bombing) and had imposed an effective blockade against Japan's home islands. It was acknowledged that for the USA to invade and secure the home islands would be an enormous task; fighting against the two million fanatical Japanese soldiers could mean up to one million allied deaths. It had been thought that *until* the home islands surrendered, there would be no end to the war with Japan. But the blockade had taken its toll as had the air-raids, and an iminent declaration of war on Japan by the USSR seemed as though Japanese morale would be rocked to the point of surrender. The USA had stipulated unconditional surrender but Japan desperately wanted to keep her Emperor and was known to be suing for peace on that basis. The USA, USSR and the United Kingdom, however, ignored these attempts to surrender. Japan's attempts could have been taken up. The USSR could have declared war against her a little earlier. Japan could have been warned of the effects of the bomb—even given a demonstration test. (The USA feared that allied prisoners would be shipped in if warning was given.) Given these circumstances, why drop the bomb? There had never apparently been any debate as to whether it should be dropped, rather when and where!

President Roosevelt had lived with the tension of the possible then the probable, but his successor President Truman turned the tension of the probable into the turbulence of the certain. Truman had set up the USA Interim Committee who, against the advice and feelings of the scientists had recommended that the bomb be dropped. The Danish nuclear physicist, Niels Bohr, had had the foresight to ask the question what happened not when the bomb was dropped but what happened to the world after the bomb was dropped. The Interim Committee was resolute in its recommendations that two targets should be chosen which hadn't been thus far severely air-bombed. That those two targets should each be both military *and* civilian targets. And that no warning should be given. A list of ten possible hits was drawn up, and the countdown to Hiroshima began.

If you're still confused about why the bomb was dropped, think about it like this. The USA now had the most destructive effective weapon known to mankind. They knew it worked, they'd invested millions of dollars into its development, but no one else yet knew the awesome effect of its destructiveness. Others were known to be investigating nuclear bombs—not least Germany, the USSR and the UK. Even Japan had her nuclear physicists. The world, the United States' military machine reckoned, had to be shown that in this field the USA led the way. And the USSR in particular had to see this. The end of Roosevelt's presidency had been marked by a series of conciliatory concessions to the USSR, but now Truman had begun quickly to ring the changes. He adopted a tough 'no-nonsense' stance with the USSR, and had begun political manoeuvering with Churchill, the British government's prime minister, to outflank any possible war spoils that might go to the USSR. You could call this attitude long-sighted. You could call it provocative. You could call it the start of the Cold War. I'd say it was probably all three. But the point is that, even taking into account the need to win a war with Japan in which America was heavily outnumbered in troop terms, the decision to bomb

Japan had as much to do with showing the USSR that the USA couldn't be messed about with. In other words, it was a political and not a military decision.

Hiroshima

Hiroshima was the seventh largest city in Japan at the time it was bombed. A thriving city, it was a mix of traditional Japan and the modern. Her citizens expected to be attacked from the air, and they had been to a limited extent, as there were troops stationed in and around the city. Emergency plans for evacuation and the destruction of 70,000 houses to make fire breaks in the city had been drawn up. But the air-raid that was to hit Hiroshima could never have been anticipated in its terrible destructiveness. And in any case, no warning was ever given. Just as President Truman's United States of America Interim Committee had recommended.

Three days of bad weather in early August 1945 had delayed the bombing of Hiroshima. Technical difficulties still abounded. The bomber to be used was the B29 Super Fortress, a massive 60-tonne unladen airplane capable of flying empty at four-hundred miles an hour. Three had crashed on take-off, loaded with dummy nuclear bombs in 'rehearsal', because of weight problems and the length of the runway at Tinian. Experiments were still being done to arm the bomb at the last possible minute (on board the plane) and thus make its transport safer. The whole nuclear bomb, from 1938 to 1945, had been a last minute 'will-it-work' affair. Now it was about to.

On 6th August the rehearsals were over. The B29 bomber, Enola Gay, carrying a crew of nine, with four scientific observers as passengers, took off from Tinian

on General Bombing Mission 13, seven tonnes over-
weight but airborne. The flight captain was Paul Tib-
bets. The Enola Gay was carrying a twenty-eight inch
diameter, ten foot long, 9,000 pound weight atomic
bomb of fissionable uranium, nicknamed 'Little Boy'.
The bomb's destructive power was 20,000 tonnes of
TNT, and it was armed on board the plane in a half-
hour operation by Captain William Parsons.

That day had dawned bright and clear over
Hiroshima, and by 8.00 am (local time) that morning
most people were on the move heading for work or
school. The air-raid sirens had already gone off twice
that morning when two United States Airforce recon-
naissance and weather planes were spotted flying high
over the city. No bombs had been dropped though, and
few people took any notice when a quarter of an hour
later at 8.15 am the sirens went off for a third and final
time as the Enola Gay, exactly on time and target, flew
over the doomed city.

'Little Boy' was released from a height of six miles at
8.15 and seventeen seconds. In the city there were even
some cheers as a small white parachute on the bomb
appeared—some thought the plane's crew were having
to bale out. But fifty-one seconds later the awful truth
became obvious as 'Little Boy' detonated at 8.16 and
eight seconds, only 200 yards from 'prime target', 1,850
feet up in the air.

In one awful instant the centre of Hiroshima was
turned into an intense two-square-mile oven. 10,000
buildings were destroyed in that area alone by the blast,
and a further 50,000 by fire. Near the centre of the
explosion people, buildings, cars, everything was
vapourised. Granite melted, stones 'wept' their cores
through the outer layers of rock, and only the shadows
of people remained outlined on the ground or on rein-

forced concrete to show where they'd been standing when vapourised. The ground's heat at the centre was later estimated at 6,000° celsius. The force of the blast, which ripped outwards across the city, carrying all before it and wiping flat 4.7 square miles, was estimated at eight tonnes per square yard. In the explosion and the fire storm which immediately followed 90% of the city's fire stations were destroyed. So were forty-two of the city's forty-five hospitals. And of Hiroshima's 298 doctors only twenty-eight survived. 1,645 of the city's 1,700 nurses didn't.

As the Enola Gay banked away from the city, a mushroom cloud 50,000 feet high shot upwards and Rear Gunner Sergeant George Canon, peering down into the cloud and inferno boiling below the plane, described it as 'like a peep into hell'. Thousands of miles away on board his yacht, President Truman, on being informed of the cataclysm which had been 'successfully' unleashed against Hiroshima, turning that city into a vast suffering pit of death, agony and misery, said, 'This is the greatest thing in history.' And God wept.

It's impossible now to be certain how many people died in the bombing of Hiroshima. Japanese estimates are of course much higher than those of the USA. In one sense, does it really matter how many thousands died? Isn't it enough that the first nuclear bomb had been dropped, without warning or precedent, and that thousands and thousands died immediately. The figures which are most likely to be accurate were between 70 and 130,000 dead, with a further 70,000 seriously injured. The United States Casualty Commission said that the total dead was 79,400, while the figure on the Hiroshima Peace Memorial Museum Monument puts the figure at 250,000 dead.

The injuries were hideous. People's features were literally melted, yet they were still alive. Ears, eyes and noses burned off, limbs mangled, bodies shredded by blast force and flying glass, or turned into one huge supturating blister by heat and radiation burns. And then the onset of radiation sickness never before seen on this earth. Blindness, bloody vomiting and diarrhoea, racking spasms and open ulcers, and later of course all the cancers and genetic defects.

And of course, as if that wasn't bad enough, it wasn't over yet. The new era was only half birthed, for with Hiroshima devastated the world's spotlight turned to Nagasaki. The Interim Committee had recommended that *two* targets be selected, and two it was to be.

Nagasaki

The Nagasaki bomb was called 'Fat Man' and was a plutonium-based device which weighed 10,000 pounds and was ten feet eight inches long. 'Fat Man' worked on a different principle to 'Little Boy' and was consequently more of a sphere than a tube in shape. This was because 'Little Boy', the Hiroshima bomb, was detonated on the 'canon' principle whereby the two pieces of material that were to be 'fissioned' were fired at one another at high speed as though from a canon. In 'Fat Man', however, the two metals were placed together like two hemispheres, then 'imploded' together within the spheroid bomb by surrounding them with carefully arranged high explosives and detonators. What matter? The bomb had, like 'Little Boy', a destructive power of 20,000 tonnes of TNT. And it would be so useful to 'field' test both types.

Three days after the Hiroshima bomb fell, the B29 bomber Bockscar, commanded by Major Sweeney, took off for its target. The original target was to have been Kokura (indeed, Nagasaki was only added to the hit list of possible cities when Kyoto was removed because of its cultural and religious significance), but bad weather here made visual bombing impossible. The bomber turned to Nagasaki. There, in a break in the clouds, Bockscar dropped her deadly cargo at 10.58 am local time, from a height of 5.3 miles, and the history of Hiroshima was repeated all over again in Nagasaki.

The city of Nagasaki had originally been founded in the sixteenth century by a Christian, and since that time had had strong religious and cultural links to Christianity. Indeed, there was a very high density of Catholic population in one quarter of the city, and it was here that the bomb fell, on the district of Urakami. Just as with Hiroshima, the air-raid sirens had sounded when the weather plane had first been spotted at 7.45 am and again at 10.53 am, but with little effect; over the war years familiarity had bred contempt.

Nagasaki had never been as ideal a target as Hiroshima. The surrounding hills meant there would be more shelter and less blast damage whereas Hiroshima had a flat plain which maximised the effects of the bomb. In fact, the military was rather disappointed that it had to be Nagasaki! However, in their favour (and against Nagasaki's), was the fact that 'Fat Man' was a 'better' bomb than 'Little Boy'. Some 36,000 people were killed and a further 40,000 seriously injured. 70% of the heavily industrialised zone was destroyed; there were 1.8 square miles of total destruction.

And with that second bomb the Interim Committee's mandate was fulfilled. President Truman was satisfied, the Russians were amazed, the British were quietly jubilant about their early role in the Bomb's development, and Japan surrendered.

But of course you and I can't leave it there. Because I said at the beginning of this chapter, we now live with the legacy of those bombings: we live in a nuclear era. Let's close this chapter with a very brief résumé of what's happened since those fateful years.

And so it goes on

Since 1945 six nuclear powers have evolved (the USA, USSR, China, France, the UK and India). They have exploded more than one thousand nuclear bombs in tests, investing more than six *trillion* dollars on arms. The most powerful of these test weapons was exploded by the USSR in their Novaya Zemlya area at 8.33 am (GMT) on the 30th October 1961. The shock wave went around the earth in thirty-six hours and twenty-seven minutes, and then went on to circle the planet another two times. The weapon had an official explosive yield of fifty-seven million tonnes of TNT. That's one-thousand four-hundred and twenty-five times the size of the Hiroshima and Nagasaki bombs put together. Some have estimated that, in fact, the device could have been much bigger—between sixty-two to ninety million tonnes of TNT. By the 16th January 1963 Krushchyov announced that the USSR had a one hundred mega-tonne bomb in East Berlin, East Germany. Such a bomb would be capable of making a crater nineteen miles in diameter and causing serious fires up to forty miles away!

The USSR joined the nuclear arms race in June 1942, but didn't obtain a nuclear chain reaction until December 1945—you can see that it's always been a near-run race. Consequently, a whole plethora of arms talks, limitation attempts and peace treaties have been developed, many of them relatively ineffective. One of the best (which unfortunately didn't work and was very much a missed opportunity) was the Baruch Plan of 1946. This would have given all nuclear weapons over into international ownership, but it was rather unfairly weighted against the Russians (being a USA proposal) who countered with their own proposal whereby all existing nuclear weapons should be destroyed and all future productions cease. What an opportunity! The USA however, with the edge on the race, refused, and directly after negotiations broke down began their extensive series of nuclear weapon tests on the Bikini Attol from the 1st July 1946 onwards.

A proliferation of pacts has followed, up to and including the SALT talks (Strategic Arms Limitation Talks) which are unique in that they are only between the two 'superpowers'—the USA and USSR. In 1987 there was an historical breakthrough in these talks; for the first time since 1945 there was actually a committed agreement to reduce existing weapons by removing one whole section of them—intermediate nuclear bombs.

However, the development of weapons has also galloped ahead. In the 1960s many missiles gained multiple warheads, thus massively increasing the nuclear stockpiles. Arsenals have grown in numbers, in destructive yield, and in accuracy. There are even hints about a weapon system called Doomsday, where a fifty thousand megatonne Cobalt Salted device has been guessed at, though never officially confirmed. Such a weapon would kill everyone and everything, except those deep underground who were prepared to stay there for more than five years.

And so it goes. It's not a history to be proud of. A weapon conceived in war, born of politics, and rapidly developing. Will it, or we, ever come to maturity? Should the Bomb be part of our world? Did the God who gave us our brains intend us to use the bomb as a war-ender or a war-deterrent? Can there ever be a justifiable nuclear war? What does God have to say about it all? What do you think?

2

So Far So Good?

Now that we've had a brief look at the history of the nuclear bomb and what it is, I'd like to spend this chapter outlining the current world situation as regards nuclear weapons. I've had to include a large number of facts and figures which are as accurate as I can make them from the research I've done. I've put these figures together in one chapter so that they're out of the way of the rest of the book, and so that you know where to find them if you want to check anything. I've found a number of contradictory figures as I've read around the subject, due either to the bias of the source or due to the estimates made on information which is difficult to obtain because of State security. I've done my best to reconcile conflicting figures where they occur.

Unfortunately, reading lists of statistics isn't the most stimulating of exercises, but I've tried to make this chapter as readable as possible. Please do stick with it, because its impact may bring home the vital need to make sure our position on the bomb is both practical and moral and biblical. The stark facts revealed in this chapter mean that we can't ignore the issue.

Since the end of the Second World War in 1945, somewhere between 10 and 20 million people have died in the wars that have raged across our globe. There have been between 130 and 200 of these wars, and in a very real sense there has been no peace since 1945 (Campaign for Nuclear Disarmament claims that 20 million have been killed in 250 wars, the United Kingdom Ministry of Defence claims 10 million in 100 wars).

Biblical peace isn't merely a cessation of fighting. It is far more positive than that, proceeding only from the heart and knowledge of God. The Hebrew word used in the Old Testament for peace is *shalom*, meaning wholeness, health and security. The Greek word used in the New Testament for peace is *sozo*, meaning healing and salvation. Peace is the power that stopped the raging of the elements when Jesus spoke the words against the storm (Mt 8:23–7), because God's peace, like His love, is powerful and positive. That kind of peace hasn't been seen around the world, where some fifteen or more wars are currently being fought.

Warfare involves vast numbers of the world's population. NATO and the Warsaw Pact countries have 12 million people in the armed forces. Around the world there are 25 million people in the forces, with a further 50 million in the paramilitary. When you include everyone involved in military research support, the total goes up to a staggering 100 million. There are 500 thousand scientists involved in military research, which is 25% of the world's total number of scientists. The United Kingdom's Ministry of Defence employs 1 million people, and half of the United Kingdom's aerospace research and one-third of the United Kingdom's electronics industry are devoted to defence. Half of *all* the research and development done in this country has direct military application.

Of course, all this has financial implications. Warfare is big business and big expenditure. The USA and USSR are spending 100 million dollars a day on defence projects. The USA spends more than double the amount that South Asia spends on the education of 300 million school children every year. What an investment! By 1979 arms spending around the world had reached 460 thousand million dollars a year (the Ministry of Defence's figures are 400 thousand million pounds per annum, and CND's figures are 500 thousand million dollars per annum). Current expenditure now stands at around 42 million pounds per hour *every* hour. That means that two weeks of global spending on defence would feed the world's hungry for a whole year. The Brandt report reveals that annual development aid costs 20 billion dollars, while annual military expenditure is around 450 billion dollars. Our longer term ten-year programme to aid food production in developing countries would only take up half of one year's world defence budget.

In 1982 the United Kingdom spent 5.3% of its gross national product (eight thousand million pounds per year) on defence, and by the end of the 1980's this is expected to rise to 7.2%. We spend more on defence than any other European country and we are one of the world's largest armaments producers, 80% of which we sell to the third world, which collectively spends more on weapons than on health and education put together. The Ministry of Defence places business worth 5 million pounds per year with 60 contractors in this country. Meanwhile the USA spends 6% of its gross national product on defence and boasts 22 thousand major corporations dealing in arms. Between 1983 and 1988, the United States planned to spend 450 thousand million dollars on their nuclear arsenal. In 1982 the

USSR spent 9% of its gross national product on defence.

The figures are mind boggling. What are all these vast sums of money actually spent on? I'd like to look quickly at the arsenals and kinds of weapons that we're talking about when it comes to 'the bomb' because, of course, there's no one bomb—this is a complex business.

Arsenals

There are two main categories of nuclear weapons— strategic and tactical or 'theatre' weapons. Strategic weapons are long-range weapons, whereas tactical are more close-range combat (and therefore more likely to be deployed in Europe). The two categories are slightly blurred by the development of intermediate weapons like the USSR's SS20, or the USA's Cruise Missile, or the European-based missile Pershing. For the first time in the history of the nuclear arms race, the USA and USSR are seeking to remove weapons from the stockpile by banning the intermediate section of nuclear weapons over something like a six-year period. A small step but in the right direction.

Let's look first at the strategic missiles. Many of these missiles have a range between 6 and 12,000 kilometres. They can carry single warheads, but recent developments mean that many of them carry several independently targeted warheads. This system is known as Multiple Independently Targetable Re-entry Vehicles, or MIRV. This means that one launched weapon can carry many missiles to different targets. These weapons are Intercontinental Balistic Missiles or ICBMs. There are also bombers which come into the long range category of strategic weapons with a range of about 12,000 kilometres. These include the USA's B52 and the USSR's Backfire bomber. These bombers can carry both freefall bombs like those dropped on Hiroshima and Nagasaki, or air-to-ground missiles like the two and a half thousand kilometre range Air Launch Cruise Missiles or ALCMs. The USA has much greater superiority in terms of bomber delivered nuclear warheads than the USSR.

Third in the category of strategic missiles after ICBMs and bombers come the Submarine-Launched Balistic Missiles (or SLBMs) with a range of about 7,000 kilometres. The USA has the submarines Poseidan and Trident I and II types. The USSR has the Delta and Typhoon types. The UK has Polaris and will soon have the Trident II submarine.

These, then, are the three main delivery systems for strategic, long-range nuclear missiles: submarine, bomber or ground-launched rocket. But what about the size of the arsenals when it comes to strategic weapons?

In 1983 the USA had 1,613 strategic ballistic missiles (1,045 ICBMs and 568 SLBMs) of which 1,118 (550 ICBMs and 568 SLBMs) are MIRVs which means that there are many more nuclear warheads than the number of weapons. The USA's bombers (274 B52's) carry 1,096 freefall nuclear bombs, 1,020 short-range missiles, and 384 air-launched cruise missiles, giving them a strike power of 2,400,000,000 tonnes of TNT. (For the purposes of this book, 1,000,000 tonnes of TNT will be referred to as a megatonne.) The B52 eight-engined 1955 bomber can carry 25 cruise missiles, each 6 metres long, weighing 1,360 kilograms with a range of about two and a half thousand kilometres and an explosive yield of 200,000 tonnes of TNT each. As America's fleet of B52 bombers is now aging, there are plans to bring in 100 newer bombers called B-1B's which will also carry the cruise missiles. The USA's submarines have 568 SLBMs which are MIRV'd to 5,200 warheads with a destructive power of 400 million tonnes of TNT. These submarines are the Poseidan type, carrying 9 MIRV'd weapons each yielding 40,000 tonnes of TNT with a range of four and a half thousand kilometres, and the Trident submarine, which is twice the size of Poseidan, carrying 8 MIRV'd nuclear weapons each with a yield of one 100,000 tonnes of TNT at a range of 7,500 kilometres. So the USA's submarines actually carry about 50% of America's strategic nuclear warheads and at any one time 20 out of the 41 submarines are ready and at sea.

All of this adds up to a horrifying total of 9,800 nuclear warheads (2,100 ICBMs, 5,200 SLBMs, and 2,500 airborn nuclear warheads) which combined have the explosive power of 4,200 million tonnes of TNT. When you see on television the devastation caused by only 20 lbs of plastic explosives in Northern Ireland, can you imagine the awesome power that we are talking about? And that's only the United States. What about the USSR?

The USSR strategic missiles are distributed in their arsenal as follows. There are 2,339 warheads altogether. 1,398 are ICBMs and 941 are SLBMs, and it's likely that a total of 1,032 of them (788 ICBMs and 244 SLBMs) are MIRV'd. These, with their 300 bombers, give a total of 7,700 actual warheads, and an explosive yield of 6,000 million tonnes of TNT.

The USSR's Delta submarines carry 12–16 SLBMs with a range of 8,000 kilometres. For example the SS-N-18 which is MIRV'd, or the SS-NX-20 with 12 warheads of 8,000 kilometres range. The Typhoon submarine is 160 metres long, weighs 25,000 tonnes, and carries 20 SLBMs. By the end of 1985 the USSR had

941 SLBMs on board 62 submarines, 244 of the SLBMs were MIRV'd giving the USSR a total of 800 nuclear warheads. At any one time 10 of these USSR submarines are ready and at sea. This means that 24% of the USSR's arsenal is on board submarines. Just 4 nuclear submarines could destroy all the major cities in the northern hemisphere—on either side!

Between them the two superpowers have approximately 15,000 strategic nuclear weapons. In addition there are the arsenals of the world's other nuclear nations. The UK nuclear strategic arsenal is based mainly around the Polaris submarine, 400 feet long and 6,000 tonnes in weight, with 16 missiles which can travel at 6,600 miles an hour over 2,875 miles. Each missile is MIRV'd to carry 3 nuclear warheads, each of which has the destructive power of 200,000 tonnes of TNT. That gives each submarine the destructive yield of nine million, 600,000 tonnes of TNT. These submarines have been in use since 1967 when they took over from the UK's defence system which at that time relied on medium-ranged bombers. There are four such submarines which undergo 10–12 week patrols, each one requiring orders from London via the Prime Minister and one of the Chiefs of Staff, to be carried out on board by two executive officers. In time of war these two executive officers on board the submarine can actually fire the nuclear weapons at their own discretion in the event of communications blackout or heavy enemy attack. In 1980 the then Conservative government made a commitment to replace the Polaris submarine with the American Trident Class I which was later to be changed in preference of the Trident Class II, with 14 times the potential firepower, to be completed by

1990 at a cost of approximately 10 billion pounds. However, the Ministry of Defence claims that Trident submarines will actually only carry two and a half times the firepower of our current Polaris submarines. Trident will account for 3 pence of every £1 spent on defence in this country. The Royal Air Force has approximately 200 nuclear capable aircraft. Then there is the artillary, or *tactical* weapons, which we will discuss shortly.

Since May 1985, France has been operating the Inflexible class of submarine, which carries 96 nuclear warheads with a four and a half thousand kilometre range, each with a 150,000 tonnes of TNT explosive yield. On average submarine launched balistic missiles take only about 15 minutes maximum to reach their targets.

Mind boggled again? The figures we've just looked at are only for the *strategic*, long-range arsenals. There's another group of nuclear weapons called tactical weapons. What about these?

There are about 25 different categories of tactical nuclear weapons. Don't worry, we're not going to go through them all! They range from artillery shells, through ground-to-ground missiles, anti aircraft shells, landmines (weighing about 70 kilogrammes) ground-, air- or submarine-based Cruise missiles, torpedoes and so on to anti submarine depth charges. These latter were probably being carried on the 'Mammoth Major' transporter which crashed in Wiltshire in January 1987. The range of land-based tactical nuclear weapons goes from about 12 kilometres to several thousand (which heads into the intermediate range of ballistic missiles) and their destructive power ranges from 10 tonnes of TNT (for the W54 landmine) to about 1 million tonnes of TNT. These types of weapons are deployed in West-

ern Europe, Asia, the USA and on the Atlantic and
Pacific fleets, and also of course in Eastern Europe by
the USSR.

Russia, for example, has the 1976 developed SS20
which has a range of 5,000 kilometres. By 1984, 60% of
the 400 such missiles in the USSR were targeted on
Western Europe, the rest on China and Asia. Each
SS20 has 3 MIRV'd heads, each with an explosive
power of 150,000 tonnes of TNT. The USSR also has
the SS21 with a range of 120 kilometres, the SS22 with a
range of 1,000 kilometres and the SS23 with a range of
500 kilometres. Meanwhile NATO has about 6,000 of
this kind of weapon. For example, the Pershing II
missile, with a guided range (RADAG) of 1,800 kilometres, and the 464 ground-launched Cruise missiles.

The United States arsenal has about 16,000 tactical
weapons compared with 10,000 strategic weapons.

OK. Let's take a breather and try and get some kind
of overview of all these figures. I will try to draw them
together and present a summary of what I've said so
far.

There are currently about 50–60,000 nuclear warheads of some description in the world, distributed
between five or six countries with nuclear arsenals. The
USA now has 26,000, and by 1990, having added
23,000 new weapons and removed 17,000 obsolete ones
(such is the nature of the race), the total will be back to
its all-time (1967) peak of 32,000 nuclear warheads.
The USSR has about the same. The United Kingdom,
France and China together have a total of about two
and a half thousand. The two superpowers have a total
explosive power of more than sixteen-thousand million
tonnes of TNT. To put it another way, more than one
million Hiroshimas, or three tonnes of TNT for every
man, woman and child on earth, or 750 times all the

high explosives ever used in war on this planet so far. To put it mildly, though appropriately, this is overkill. Even as I sit writing this more news is coming in of the USA's and USSR's determination to remove all inter-mediate-range missiles such as Pershing and Cruise. Yet the arms race continues to escalate (Star Wars, strategic weapons, etc)—and has done ever since 1945. But the problem is, *can* there be a winner in this race? If these are the arsenals of today, what will developments mean for tomorrow? Because a race, of course, is never static.

Developments

First we need to mention those countries which are developing their own capability to become nuclear nations with the potential both to make, store and deliver nuclear weapons. A number of countries already have nuclear power programmes but as yet no nuclear warfare capability, although the step between the two is a relatively short one. So although at present there are five nuclear nations, there are a further nine developing or about to enter the race. These are Argentina, West Germany, The Netherlands, Japan, India, Israel, South Africa, Pakistan and Egypt. What's more, there are a further five on the threshold of developing a nuclear programme of defence (Brazil, Iraq, Libya, South Korea and Taiwan) which gives a total of nine-teen soon to enter the race in full. It is thought that by the end of the century the number of nations in the nuclear club will be about a hundred. The risk of nuclear warfare or accident is therefore rising (I hesi-tate to say developing) all the time.

Then there's the development of the weapons and systems themselves. By 1990 the USA will have scrapped 17,000 obsolete weapons, so great is the turn-over of technological development. They will, however, have added 23,000 new ones. The main development at present is in terms not of explosive power, since as I've already indicated the current global situation is one of global overkill, but rather in terms of accuracy. The accuracy of nuclear bombs is measured by their Circular Error Probability or CEP. This is the radius of the circle centred on your target within which half of your missiles can be reasonably expected to fall. The CEP of many missiles is falling (ie, becoming more accurate) all the time with the advancement of guidance systems. For example, the USA's Minuteman III ICBM (there are 550 of them) has a CEP of only 200 metres at a range of 8,000 miles and an explosive yield of between 170,000 to 350,000 tonnes. This is a development of the Minuteman II (there are 450 of these) which, with a speed of 14,000 miles per hour, has a range of 7,000 miles. The USA's Titan II ICBM (there are 52 of them) is 'better' than Titan I, as it now has a speed of 17,000 miles per hour and a range of 9,300 miles. Then there's the USA's NX system which will have a CEP of 100 metres.

The West is not alone in its developments. The USSR's SS18 ICBM has a CEP of 400 metres, but that will soon be reduced to 250 metres. Each of these warheads will have an explosive power of 500,000 tonnes of TNT. Should the Russians so choose the SS18 is capable of carrying the world's largest nuclear warhead with an explosive yield of 20,000 million tonnes of TNT. In a similar way the SS19 ICBM is being 'improved' and both the SS18 and SS19 are being MIRV'd to carry 6–8 or 10 warheads. So is the older SS17 ICBM which will carry 4 warheads of 750,000 tonnes of TNT explosive power. And so the development goes on. More warheads. Higher 'yield'. Greater accuracy.

Meanwhile intelligence gathering systems related to measuring the arms race (or verifying the dismantling and disarmament of nuclear weapons) from space through satellites has also developed. Both the USA and the USSR have such systems. The USA also has the potential reusable launcher in the form of the shuttle which is not only for space investigation and experimentation but also for military use. The USSR has the edge on the USA with an anti-satellite system (ASAT). And, of course, there's the famous Strategic Defence Initiative (SDI or 'Star Wars') from the USA, which went public in 1983. This is a defence system which aims to destroy Intercontinental Ballistic Missiles before they reach their target, thus rendering much of the enemy's nuclear strike forces useless, while retaining the USA's own ability to strike.

With the development and expansion of the arms race comes the increased possibility of nuclear accidents, as technology becomes more and more complex and as the sheer numbers of weapons, systems and countries involved increases. Some near misses have been very well reported, as in the Cuban missile crisis of October 1962 when the world trembled on the brink of nuclear holocaust. This infamous stand off occured at the Bay of Pigs, when Russian warships carrying nuclear weapons which they were attempting to place in Cuba were stopped by the USA's ships under President Kennedy's orders and the whole United States Military procedure was activated to red alert.

That hasn't been the only time that the world has come to the brink of nuclear war. On 9th November 1979 an incident occurred involving computer tape which was used in the tactical 'war games' which both sides play to develop strategy in the context of theoretical war scenarios. These war scenarios prepare either side for the possible outcomes of all out or limited nuclear war. By accident this particular tape was presented through the USA's defence computers as though the theoretical scenario was actually a real situation. For the three to six minutes which it took the back up fail safe systems to check what was happening (the back up systems fortunately *did* work), the USA's computers were telling Strategic Air Command that ICBM's had been launched against America by the USSR. Fortunately no retalitory moves were made; a submarine launched missile off the east coast of America would hit Washington within 5 minutes—in the nuclear arms race there is little time for errors.

The same thing happened again on 3rd June 1980, and once again on 6th June 1980 until eventually the fault was traced to an incorrect computer microchip which had cost a mere 46 cents! How ironic if that faulty and so cheap chip had brought about a worldwide nuclear holocaust when billions of pounds are spent on defence and deterrents. We came to the brink, but didn't quite go over.

Then there was the explosion in an Intercontinental Ballistic Missile silo in the USA on 18th September 1980. This (unofficially) sent a Titan nuclear warhead several hundred yards through the air from the silo to land in a nearby field. It also wrenched off the 750 tonne silo door and left a 250 foot crater. The explosion was triggered by a chance accident—a spanner dropped from a height of 70 feet. What about the false alarms which include flights of geese crossing radar fields, or even mere shadows from the moon triggering the system? In the 1970s the USA Pentagon estimated that each of its early warning systems gave a false signal up to four times a year. Random failures in air-defence computers are currently probably running at about two to three a year. In a recent eighteen month period the USA logged 147 false alarms. In the event of even a limited nuclear war the electromagnetic storms caused could quite easily trigger more electrical computer and radar errors or communication blocks that would lead to the launching of further missiles. And so it gets worse. The accidents are not confined to the USA. If they happen there they will also be happening in the USSR, and probably on a greater scale since computer technology there is acknowledged on a worldwide scale to be behind that of America.

Not all accidents are caused by computer error. In January 1987 the dangers of nuclear warhead convoys were dramatically illustrated when two 'Mammoth Majors' from the Royal Naval Armaments Depot, Dene Hill, collided on an icy Wiltshire road. One of the transporters was 'probably' loaded with nuclear depth charges and it left the road to overturn in a field, while the other poised overhanging an embankment. The recovery operation for the vehicle in the field took eighteen hours. Nor was this an isolated incident; there have been others. With nuclear warheads being carried weekly on the countries busiest and most dangerous motorway, the M25 around London (where you're ten times more likely to have a road accident than anywhere else in the UK), there will be others. This type of accident obviously involves the human element, and indeed any computer is only as good as its operator. The pressure and therefore failure rate which can be put down to 'human error' is fearsome, and carries *at least* equally fearful implications. In the early 1970s some 200,000 people in the USA alone carried this kind of nuclear responsibility, and 3,650 of them were dismissed because of mental, alcohol or drug instability or indiscipline.

These factors combine to make the possibility of accidental nuclear war a very real one, and they make the possibility of a 'launch on warning' system currently being discussed appear truly horrifying. For if a nuclear bomb were to be launched by accident then under that policy full-scale retribution would occur from the country that was accidentally hit and before we know it we would be involved in nuclear holocaust. As long as the arms race proliferates, so too does the possibility of one of these accidents having global consequences. And even that last phrase is jargon: 'global consequences' could mean the end of the world.

After a while all the facts and figures become rather numbing. So let's try to get those figures back into human proportion (or should I say 'inhuman' proportion?) by looking at the awesome destructive power of the weapons we have been talking about.

The IRA uses between 5 lbs to 200 lbs of explosives (usually based on a mixture of chemical compounds and fertilisers, though occasionally plastic explosives are used) in its bombs in Northern Ireland and in its bombing sallies on the mainland. Five pounds will blow open all the doors, boot and bonnet of a car if that's the target. Two hundred pounds will destroy a whole building and badly damage neighbouring buildings, smashing all the windows in the streets around. The tactical (that is battlefield and smaller) nuclear warheads that we've been listing range from about 10 tonnes of TNT (which is a very high explosive) to 1,000,000 tonnes of TNT, that's 22,400 lbs to 2,240 *million* pounds of TNT! The largest warhead at present is the ICBM 20 megaton warhead carrying 20 million tonnes of TNT which is a staggering 44,800 million pounds of TNT or 2,240 *million* IRA bombs of 200 lbs each. And that's one warhead.

The destructive power of these weapons isn't just confined to the blast and heat and fireball as it would be in a conventional bomb, bad enough though that would be. With nuclear weapons comes the horror of immediate and then long-term radiation sickness and death, the ecological dangers of fall-out, and the slow killer of radiation enhanced cancers and genetic disorders. For example, after the nuclear bomb which was dropped on Hiroshima in 1945, the observable instance of cancer-related deaths in that city had increased thirty times by the 1950s.

Reliable estimates and tests indicate what the results would be of nuclear explosions over our cities and countries, given today's more accurate and more powerful weapons. It needs to be noted that many modern nuclear warheads are deliberately 'dirty' weapons, that is they are created to have a high fall-out factor. This is done by encasing the fusion bomb of uranium 235 in uranium 238. Uranium 235 has a half-life (that is the period of time which the nuclear material will take to décay to half its original radioactive state) of 700 million years! Fall-out is dust which has been sucked up by the explosion and made radioactive, and its effects can be very long term indeed: we are still getting some fall-out from atomic tests made by the United States and USSR in the 1950s and 1960s. Fall-out can also depend on very variable factors. Weather can wreak havoc: rain or snow will increase fall-out effects eight times more than if the weather was dry and fine. Wind will determine where and how far clouds of radioactive fallout will drift. As a rough guide, every 2,000 tonnes of energy released in a nuclear explosion will produce 2 lbs of fall-out material, involving some ninety or more radioactive materials.

What happens in a nuclear explosion in terms of destructive power? Well, in a millionth of a second a temperature is reached of eighteen million degrees farenheit, which is hotter than the inside of our sun, and this temperature then expands to form a colossal fireball. With a 10 megaton weapon the fireball alone will be up to three and a half miles wide. Next for up to a minute energy will be released in all directions. This energy comes in the form of heat (that actually caters for one-third of the energy released), light (mainly ultraviolet and infrared light which means that the light is actually brighter than it appears causing many instances of blindness), sound, blast (travelling at 750 miles an hour) and, of course, radiation. A mushroom cloud would shoot upwards at speeds in excess of 300 miles an hour. From such an explosion (10 megaton) a crater 180 feet deep and 9 square miles wide would be formed and irreparable damage would be caused over 360 square miles. The chart overleaf gives some indication of the effects of such 10 megaton blast, though allowance needs to be made for variable factors already mentioned such as the weather, the height at which the weapon is detonated above the ground, and the contours of the land over which it is exploded, the structure of buildings, etc.

Take another scenario. In the 1979 report *The Effects of Nuclear War*, the USA Congress estimated that a 1 megaton explosion on a large American city would immediately leave 2 million dead and 1 million seriously injured with little chance of medicinal aid. It further estimated that in an attack first by the USSR followed by retaliation from the USA, casualties would be an immediate 160 million American dead and 100

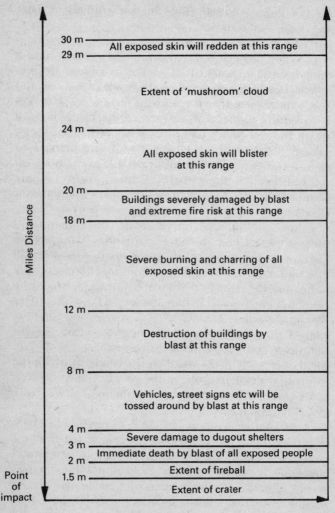

**The effects of a 10 megatonne nuclear blast
in all directions from point of impact.**

million Russian dead. These figures are based on an attack against military and economic targets, not civilian ones. Economic targets are listed in priority and one of the eight critical industries to be attacked would be the pharmaceutical industry—what price medicine (or doctors) in the event of nuclear attack and attempted survival? At present the USA can cater for some 2,000 severe burns cases; in the event of an all-out nuclear attack the number of such cases would probably be 25 million. Should the attack be limited to military targets alone the figures are reduced; 20 million immediate deaths in the USA and 10 million (because of a smaller population which is more sparsely distributed) in the USSR.

If, however, the attack were all out, then the figures become 190 million American deaths and 130 million Russian deaths. It needs no mathematician to work out that we are talking mass genocide. Three hundred and twenty million dead in the event of such war. You can't even imagine such carnage, so many individuals burned, blown and blasted away. So many families, homes, cars, industries, towns, cities, states, totally destroyed. All those hopes, dreams, fears, memories. All those thoughts, achievements. All that art, literature, history. All gone.

The death toll wouldn't stop at the immediate casualties. It's estimated that following a nuclear attack on the USA that avoided population targets, cancer deaths over the next 40 years would be in the millions. A large nuclear exchange would cause up to 6 million natural spontaneous abortions in the USA alone, with a further 8 million in the USSR and five million in other countries, leaving for future generations the inheritance of 36 million mutations whose effects would be felt over the next thirty generations.

With the deaths and injuries would go the large-scale destruction of sanitation, industry, agriculture, medicine and government. The environment would be terribly affected, with a strong possibility of a fall-out cloud causing a nuclear ice-age and the ozone layer over the northern hemisphere of the world being reduced by between 30% and 70%. And that would be after only a 50% all-out nuclear war. The reduction in the ozone layer alone would result in many more deaths from burns and cancers. And the natural ecological chain would be severely disrupted and unbalanced. For example, birds would be destroyed, but insects, whose natural resistance to radiation levels is much higher, wouldn't be destroyed, with dreadful results on any remaining crops.

In many countries, including most which don't have nuclear weapons, there are nuclear power stations which in the event of war become both prime targets and sources of dreadful destruction. A 1,000 megawatt nuclear plant, for example, has as much radioactive material as 1,000 Hiroshima bombs, with potential disastrous results in terms of fall-out, as was seen in 1986 with a very small-scale incident at the USSR power plant at Chernobyl.

The cataclysm we are anticipating clearly has world-wide implications so you'd expect the picture to be little better in the United Kingdom. On the scale of attack presumed in the UK government civil defence exercise Operation Square Leg (September 1980), an estimate was made of the effects of four nuclear warheads hitting London with two others landing nearby, giving a total destructive power of 200 megatons. The results indicated that within three months of the attack more than 5 million would be dead. Yet it's likely—at least as long as Cruise missiles are based around London (and it will take six years for the agreements reached in September 1987 between the USSR and the USA to come into effect and remove intermediate missiles such as Cruise and Pershing)—that the city would be targeted by 1,000 megatons of nuclear destructive power. That's the equivalent of 65,000 Hiroshimas unleashed on Britain's capital, which after Cruise will remain a military and governmental target.

None of this is exactly inspiring stuff, but it does give a nightmarish glimpse of the size of the problem. It's not a subject you can afford to be woolly minded over. Nor is it a subject you can afford to think about later. There may not be a later. And it's not a subject that God has no opinion over. The implications of effects on young people (and on older people) are enormous, as we'll see in the next chapter. In the face of such issues I believe there are biblical, practical, workable absolutes, which we'll examine later. But if you've stuck with this chapter so far, stay with me for one final section where we'll consider the current policies that govern the instruments of absolute destruction.

The situation is a complex overlap of evolving policies, countries and pacts. I think the simplest way of explaining current policy is to look at where we've come from, where we're at currently, and on to speculate about where we seem to be heading.

We've seen from the previous chapter that in 1945, despite pressure from the USSR and experimentation within Germany, the USA was alone in its implementation of the nuclear programme which led to viable nuclear bombs. So at that stage policy was easy. But as countries began to experiment and tests were made on nuclear explosions so there came about a proliferation of treaties and pacts and the beginning of the arms race as we know it which of course led to the need for the development of nuclear war policies.

The original policy was quite a simple one. At this stage of the arms race you were winning by increasing the number, size and range of your weapons. Though the number could only be increased by adding to your arsenal of rockets, as MIRV'd weapons weren't yet technically feasible. This meant that more and more targets were added. Since technology at this point couldn't deliver a nuclear warhead onto smaller *military* targets with any large degree of success, nor even muster the surveillance techniques to *spot* those military targets, these multiple targets tended to be centres of population which were quite easily targeted and large enough to justify the massive explosive power of the original long-range ICBMs, which were the birth of the strategic class of nuclear weapon.

The policy which evolved from this part of the arms race was quite simple, as I've already said. 'You fire at our cities and we'll fire at yours' and no one wins because nothing's left. This policy was known appropriately as Mutually Assured Destruction, frequently shortened to MAD(!). This policy has been the basis for the arms race for NATO, the USSR and the USA *officially* ever since.

However, since as early as 1960 the Pentagon began to look at the possibility of moving from MAD towards city-for-city counterstrikes, then as accuracy of surveillance and targeting increased, policy began to move toward targeting only military and/or economic centres. The idea of 'winning' a nuclear war seemed more possible, and therefore more attractive. From there it's only a short step to the idea of making your first strike successful by wiping out the enemy's ability to counterstrike, and so you develop a 'first-strike policy' (which NATO have actually refused) instead of Mutually Assured Destruction. And *then*, because *either* side might have such a policy, you also develop a 'strike on warning' policy because you can't risk the enemy wiping out your ability to retaliate by their first strike.

Now all these policies have been actively looked at though officially denied. The indications, however, are there for all to see. The Pentagon has its Single Integrated Operational Plan (SIOP) to destroy the enemy's war-making capabilities. The shift by the super powers toward more accurate lower yield weapons does reflect this hidden policy of 'winning' a nuclear war. So we have mobile bases for more accurate missiles, such as ground launched Cruise missiles, etc. Then in 1980 President Carter signed Presidential Directive No 59, with its call for 'flexibility in targeting'.

In Europe, where East faces West eyeball to eyeball, the idea of limited nuclear warfare also looms large, hence the growth of tactical nuclear weapons. Europe is the 'theatre' for this scenario of nuclear exchange, and it is here that the neutron bomb is likely to be deployed. This is the ultimate in absurd reversed values, as the bomb can kill people but leave property standing. If the Star Wars programme becomes operative, the USA would be able to target anything in the USSR with little fear of nuclear retaliation.

The point about the existing policy is obvious and important. I want to look at the whole issue of deterrents in a later chapter, but suffice it to say at this point that deterrents only work if both sides have roughly equal capability to inflict terror and destruction upon each other. Only let one side think it can 'win' a nuclear war (and we've looked at figures on the cost of such a 'win' in human lives) and the war becomes all the more likely. If it's thought to be 'winnable' someone is going to want to fight it. If you'll permit me phrasing it emotively (it's an emotive issue) current nuclear war policy was shifted from mutual suicide to mass murder without the guarantee of non-escalation to global anni-hilation.

And that's the current situation.

3

Look to the Future

According to a survey done in April 1987 for a top national Sunday magazine the two greatest fears shared by more than 1,000 representatives of today's teenage generation are first unemployment, and secondly nuclear holocaust. Two fears—one personal, one global. Both real possibilities. Both real fears.

When I grew up in the 1960s in a semi-rural part of England neither of these were big fears. Unemployment and nuclear war were certainly possibilities, but not probabilities. There were 'ban the bomb' campaigns and marches on Aldermaston and some politicians like Michael Foot made their names around the attendant publicity. But it was only an issue, not an oppressive fear affecting most people. No one then had ever heard of Bruce Kent, and cruise meant a holiday on the Norfolk Broads!

Today the threat of nuclear war is both real and immediate. And nowhere is this threat, with potential genocide, annihilation, holocaust and the horrors of unlikely survival, felt more keenly than by young people. At no time in the history of the world has a likelihood of total destruction been more probable, and the following generations inherit a worsening situation. The legacy of previous generations is one of tension, fear and threat. And you, the inheritors, the young people of today, have the most to lose. It's your hopes, dreams and ambitions, unlived and unrealised, that may never happen, where others before you have had their chance. It's you who will be the unwilling victims of older but not wiser statesmen. Should the button be pushed, it will not be the young generation who decide to push it, though it will be the young who have the greatest chance of survival, and who therefore must contend with the horrors of that survival.

If all that sounds rather bleak, it's because it reflects the tremendous fear, bitterness and insecurity that I find among young people on the whole subject of the bomb. As I travel around the country talking to young people in schools, colleges, universities, prisons, on the streets and in churches, I find an almost fatalistic expectation that within this current youth generation there will be a holocaust, be it accidental or deliberate. The scenes of warfare played out against the backdrop of the Middle East or the Gulf tend no longer to be isolated instances and evidence of the greed of man, but could at any given moment flare into international confrontation, particularly between the two superpowers, the USA and USSR. The scenario is depressing because, like some Sword of Damocles it hangs over the heads of young people, causing pressure and fear. Pressure without outlets, pressure with no apparent sign of change, is pressure that leads to depression. The scenario is also demoralising, because along with the other great fear of unemployment, the nuclear threat puts a great black fullstop to all hopes, aims and aspirations. Morale goes out of the window in the face of potential

annihilation. 'What's the point?' is the long-term question asked by a youth generation which doesn't believe
the world, let alone themselves, has a future. And the
scenario is dehumanising, because individuals are swal-
lowed by an arms race that sees people as target populations, and sacrifices morality to base instincts for
survival should a bomb ever be dropped. Though it's
not the sole cause, I am convinced that the nuclear
threat is one factor in the massive upsurge in teenage
depression in the 1980s, and the consequent increase in
teenage suicides, particularly thirteen to eighteen year
olds, as reported in 1987 by The Samaritans, the tele-
phone counselling organisation.

The question for us in this chapter is, although we
know there is cause for alarm and concern, what does
the Bible say about expecting and therefore the fear of
nuclear annihilation? In this chapter I'd like to begin to
develop my approach to the issue of Christians and the
bomb, before looking later in the book at other
approaches.

In approaching this issue, it's vital that we don't
allow tension and fear to pressurise us into mere reaction, otherwise we will be in danger of altering our
conclusions to suit the circumstances. We must at all
costs avoid situational ethics ('If they shoot/bomb us,
can we shoot/bomb them back?'). Instead we must look
for biblical positive alternatives.

Does the Bible give us a perspective on this question
of nuclear annihilation? I believe it gives outlines about
the end of time which reduce much fear and anxiety for
Christians. It's reassuring to me to read that God, in
addition to Greenpeace, the Campaign for Nuclear Disarmament, the British Labour Party, the USSR and
USA, etc, has a view to express on the nature of the

world's end. And given the option, I think I'd rather opt for God's forecast rather than theirs.

The Bible clearly states that Jesus Christ is coming again to this earth. Christians have differed for centuries over when and how he'll come, but all agree, as it's clear in Scripture, that come again he will. I remember how a friend of mine on his wedding anniversary took his wife out to a restaurant for a romantic dinner for two. They were both rather hard up at that time so they ordered a fish course. They had just begun it when my friend's wife, who was facing the door, nudged my friend under the table. A businessman had entered, resplendent in bowler hat and pin-striped suit, with furled umbrella and a leather case, and a copy of *The Times* under his arm, red carnation—the works! He sat down at a reserved table for one just opposite my friends, and proceeded to order the most mouth-watering meal imaginable! White wine with smoked salmon starter, followed by red wine with a mixed salad, vegetable selection and a huge T-bone steak. But the oddest thing was, this city gent ate his meal in sections. That is, he ate the salad first, then the mixed veg, then the potatoes. And then, just as he was about to saw into this massive juicy succulent steak, he looked up with a glazed expression on his face, his jaw dropped, his mouth opened, and my friend said he did what could only be described as 'smote himself on the forehead' as though he had a brainwave, or just remembered that he'd forgotten something. Leeping to his feet, this immaculate bloke grabbed his bowler, brolly, brief case and paper and legged it through the door without paying.

My friend looked at his wife. She looked at him. Neither spoke. They looked across at the steak. It looked very lonely left on the man's plate! Another pause. Then my friend reached across, skewered the steak with his fork, and the two of them began to share it. Never, apparently, has steak tasted so good! And five minutes later, as the last mouthful was being raised to their mouths, the wife went bright red, her eyes stared in horror at my friend, who turned in his seat to see the city gent come back in through the restaurant door! They thought he'd gone for good, they hadn't expected him back, but...

Do you see the point? The Man is coming back! Believe it or not, understand it or not, expect it you probably won't, but the Man is coming back! The teaching on the Second Coming is spread throughout both the Old and New Testaments. You'll find it in Isaiah, Daniel, Joel and Malachi. It's there in Matthew, Mark, Luke and John, in 1 and 2 Corinthians, 2 Thessalonians and Revelation. There's no doubt about it: Jesus Christ is coming back to earth. The New Testament has to use three key words in Greek to describe his return properly. Together these words paint an important picture of what that return will be like. It's important because a lot of us might be wondering if there'll be anything left to return to!

The first Greek word is *parousia*. This means that Jesus Christ will be heralded back as a ruler, a potentate, a king. It's a word that might describe the pomp and ceremony and majesty attending say the visit of our Monarch to a Commonwealth country. It's a word full of authority and power. It will be no child in a smelly cow box in a damp cave this time round, but a King coming to establish his kingdom in fullness.

The second word which is used is *apokalypsis* referring to the demonstration or revelation of something previously hidden or partially obscured. It's like the sun peeping out from behind storm clouds. So on Jesus

Christ's second visit he will be revealed to all and every knee will have to bow to him as Lord, not just those who do so now willingly (Phil 2:10–11).

Thirdly comes the word *epiphaneia* which refers to a visible, physical reappearance or return, coming again, a second coming. This is not going to be a mystical return but a very real and practical one.

Now, the combination of these descriptions of the Second Coming of Jesus Christ gives a clear picture with implications for the earth he is returning to. He will come as a king, revealed in all his power and glory to everyone. His return will be a physical reality, not something spiritual seen by the 'eye of faith'. The implications? There *will* be a kingdom for the king to return to—earth. There will be a people for Jesus to be king over—no total annihilation. And he is coming, a physical resurrected Lord, to a physical world. The Bible implies that even as 'final judgment', a global holocaust resulting in total annihilation will not happen.

However, moving on a stage, there is also a clear indication in Scripture that in the last days there will be a time of terrible conflict. The Bible calls this a 'tribulation' which will set family against family, nation against nation, when many will wish they hadn't been born and the faith of many will fail. Matthew chapter 24 makes all this quite plain. This tribulation will be marked by certain clearly identifiable signs, many of which we can now see. The Bible states that no one knows for sure when the end times are with us. Even Jesus himself said that that information had been reserved for God alone; Jesus Christ didn't know it! Every generation since Jesus' day has thought that they were living in the last days and expected Jesus Christ to return very soon. One thing is for sure though, every generation which believes that it is living in the last days and will see Christ's return is *nearer* the truth than the last one. The news is this; for *you* this *is* the last generation! You only get the one.

This coming tribulation will be largely under the direction of a political, economic and religious leader who will dominate world affairs and demand total submission, which includes worship. He will have supernatural satanic powers and this is described in the Bible in various ways: 'the abomination that causes desolation' (Mt 24:15), 'the man of lawlessness' (2 Thess 2:3), 'antiChrist' (1 Jn 2:18 etc), and 'the beast' (Rev 13). These are the references behind a spate of sensational but dangerous occult films in the 1970s and early 1980s such as *The Omen, Omen II, Damien* etc.

I have to say that I can find no biblical backing for the theory referred to as 'the secret rapture'. This theory says that Christians are snatched out of this world before the tribulation and Jesus Christ's subsequent reign called the Millenium). The idea of a 'secret rapture' has the danger of making Christians feel smug: it'll work out ok for us, sorry about you! This in turn can lead to apathy or a survivalist mentality whereby we don't really care either for our world or for other people other than to see them as evangelistic targets. This seems to me to run against what the Bible teaches about advancing God's kingdom aggressively through faith (Mt 11:12), and carefully looking after our world (Gen 1:28–31) and caring for other people.

After the tribulation and Second Coming of Christ is the final judgment and the resurrection of the dead, with those still alive at Jesus Christ's coming being changed instantly (without dying) into their resurrection bodies which are recognisable but imperishable and for God's glory (1 Cor 15:35–58). The Christian's destiny is not one of disembodied spirits floating around cotton-wool clouds, but a new heaven and a new earth and a new resurrection body (Rev 21, 1 Cor 15) where there will be no pain, no sorrow, or tears.

God is currently forming this new creation. Originally he started with the universe, then he made the earth and lastly people (Gen 1). This time round he's started first with people (2 Cor 5:15) and will finish with a new heaven and earth, like one big mirror image. The central point of this re-creation and of course the Bible itself is Jesus Christ. He is the means of new birth and new life. He is the One who keeps everything going (Col 1:17). He is the pivotal point of history (his story).

What perspective does this brief look at the Bible give us about the nuclear threat? Well, whatever the timescale of whatever happens before this recreation is completed, we know that as Christians, God can give us grace, strength and courage. And what's more we will win through in the end! There will be an earth and people for Jesus Christ to return to. God has never allowed total annihilation to happen; even with the Flood in Noah's days, God saved eight people and vowed never to flood the earth again (Gen 6:18, 9:12–17). Now, after Jesus' birth, life, death and resurrection, we have the far better covenant of God's grace, love and forgiveness through Jesus to cope with mankind's sin.

Nonetheless, we are still faced with a potentially horrendous world situation through the nuclear bomb. Our biblical survey above should give a framework for action not an excuse for complacency or sinful apathy. For the reality is that, together with the truth of that biblical scenario, is the world as we know it with its nuclear threat, and the indication in 2 Peter chapter 3 of some kind of massive scale disaster (presumably that which Jesus was referring to in Matthew chapter 24).

I'd like to explain further this idea of the future we have to look forward to as Christians. Stick with me, because how you view this effects how you live now. What we believe affects the way we live; our faith for the future affects our security for the present; our security for the present enables us to walk free from the past.

If you were to ask most people in this country (approximately 76% of adults and up to 80% of young people) if they believe in God, they would answer yes. Most people believe that there is a God somewhere behind everything, but to them he is remote, unknowable, and doesn't affect the way they live. Most people would say that this God is not the God of organised religion (I'd have a lot of sympathy with them!) and most would reject any idea that such a God would make moral claims on their lives. The word used to describe this kind of understanding of God is deism. The god of deism is little more than a force behind the universe, the 'force' of a 'Star Wars' film and not a personal God who intervenes in our world.

The God of the Bible, is both personal, active and one who intervenes. He is called Emmanuel—'God with us'. He hasn't created the universe and then left it like a clock to run down into chaos while he sits remotely in some corner totally uninvolved. No, the God of the Bible continues to be involved in all that happens to his universe; to hurt with the hurting, to be angry with injustice, to rejoice with the happy. The Word used to describe this understanding of God is theism. Our God has a character, personality, will and emotions (that's why we have these things—we are made in God's image [Gen 1:26]). So we have a God who can be grieved. Who can laugh, dance, whistle, clap, sing, even run with joy over his children.

This Christian revelation of God is unique among all the world's religions. Creation reflects God's energy, joy and love which overflowed from the relationship of Father, Son and Holy Spirit into a great, vivid splash of perfect universe. In this universe all things were made good, and you and I, God's pinnacle of creation, made in his image, were proclaimed by him to be *very* good (Gen 1:31).

When we chose to disobey God, we took with us in our fall the whole of creation and creativity. So now creation is no longer perfect but suffers under drought, earthquake, disease, etc (Rom 8:18–22). Even the animal kingdom evidences the violent results of our fall from friendship with our Creator: as the poet Tennyson put it, 'Nature, red in tooth and claw.'

The Bible's clear teaching on the future had four emphases, and we have to hold all of them in balance in order to see the full picture. Lose any of these emphases and your reaction to the threat of nuclear war may be extreme, whether extreme fear or extreme apathy. Before people like you and I rejected God (in the same way that many still do), the creation was God's territory. But whose is it now? President Bush's? Gorbachov's? Thatcher's? Their successors?

Well, first the world continues to be God's world because He created it and has never let go of it. He is not a remote, uninterested force, but an active, personal God, totally involved in the world—and in all its joys and griefs.

Secondly, the world is also Satan's world because he has corrupted it. Satan really is about; he's powerful and he's your enemy. God cares for you individually, but Satan only wants to harm you because you represent potential for God. Satan hates the image of God in people (all people, saved or not, are made in God's image; every good gift comes from God [Jas 1:17]), and so he tries increasingly to destroy God's image within you. The way he tries to do this is through corruption—unlike God, he is a created being, so he does not have the same kind of creative powers as God. The Flood, Abraham's doubting of God, the Egyptian slaughter of Israelite children, and Herod's similar attack on children in the New Testament—all were Satan's attempt to destroy the blood-line from Adam through the Jewish people, because eventually it led to Jesus Christ Himself who would make it possible for people to be saved and have God's image fully restored in them.

Now, however evil and powerful Satan is, he is still created and not creator. He is not the equal and opposite of God, as though the universe was perpetually in the grip of some giant sea-saw! Now God's on top...oops!...Now Satan's on top! But what God makes good, Satan corrupts. God made sex and Satan corrupted it to lust. God made appetite and Satan corrupted it to greed. God made beauty, Satan encourage vanity. Medicine—Euthenasia. Contraception—abortion. Some might argue nuclear weapons are a corruption of the God-given potential power in nuclear power. And so on and so on.

Satan has taken over territory in this world wherever people have chosen to give him legal access, for Satan is a legalist. Open a door to him and you can be sure he'll enter. Fall down and you can be sure he'll put the boot in—he's no Queensberry Rules gentleman fighter, but a street brawler. Build a landing-strip of sin in your life, and Satan will land on it. So the Bible calls him the god of this world, and the prince of this world, but not the King. For the King is Jesus (Jn 14:30; 2 Cor 4:4).

Thirdly, the Bible is clear about Satan having been already defeated, because it teaches that this world is Jesus' world because he has conquered it (Col 2:13–15). There are many references in the Bible to Jesus as the Captain of God's army. Satan was defeated historically in world and human history, 2,000 years and 4,000 miles away, when Jesus Christ died on the cross at a skull-like rock called Golgotha outside a Middle Eastern city called Jerusalem. In spiritual reality, when Jesus physically died on the cross, he leapt into hell and stomped on the neck of Satan, taking from him for ever the power of death and separation from God, and forging a way by which our sins could be paid for and forgiveness.

But there's more! The fourth and final thing the Bible teaches is that this world is our world because Jesus commissioned us (Mt 28:18–20). Having thought that Satan had defeated Jesus by getting him to the cross, Satan is now horrified to discover that through the power of the Holy Spirit of God there are now millions (84,000 more each day) of 'little Christ's' (that's what the word 'Christian' means), and they are scattered all around the world! Millions taking seriously the command of God, through Jesus Christ, to make disciples and give God His world back. We are God's mop-up squad between D-day (the death, resurrection and ascension of Jesus Christ) and V-day (his return). The implications for how we live individually and together are massive. As members of the body of Jesus Christ the government of God's kingdom has been given to us, the shoulders of that body, with Jesus Christ as the head (Is 9:6) and within society, as salt and light, the church becomes an agent for the kingdom of God. So let's get it right now.

God is still involved. Jesus has won the right against

Satan for you and I to take care of the earth and have good relationships with God and with others. When Jesus saves you he 'redeems' you, buys you back as an individual, to receive wholeness (remember, the Greek New Testament word *sozo* means salvation, healing, wholeness and is the equivalent of the Old Testament Hebrew word *shalom* which means peace, health and wholeness). God wants to extend wholeness over societies, over nations, over all ethnic groupings and peoples (Mt 28:19). Evangelism is much bigger than the salvation of individual souls—though it starts there. It is the extending of God's kingdom through the church.

What exactly *is* this kingdom? Well, even Jesus Christ had problems with that one! He had to cast around to find a suitable analogy. 'To what,' he said, 'shall I compare this kingdom?' (Lk 13:20). An earthly kingdom has a king, a people and a territory. Jesus said that the kingdom of God is rather like this earthly kingdom, except that it is within us. In the kingdom of God, Jesus is the king, Christians are the people, and the territory is wherever we allow Jesus to be king in our lives as individuals and a society. Jesus explained that we live between times, in a kind of interface between the kingdom of God which has already come with him, and the fullness of the kingdom of God which is 'at hand' (so reach out and grab a slice! It's not 'pie in the sky when you die', but 'steak on a plate while you wait' [Mt 4:17]). This kingdom will only fully be here when Jesus comes again. It's kingdom come *and* coming.

So Jesus Christ builds his church (Mt 16:18) and you and I as part of his Church seek the kingdom (Mt 6:33). But the reality is that most of us are too busy naval gazing, spiritually speaking, trying to build the church with structures or pastoral systems until we're all mothered and smothered instead of aggressively seeking the kingdom. We've let the Communists steal the biblical reality of a kingdom here on earth, while we've settled for a Utopia in the sky, a future reward that all too often either blackmails people or sinks them into apathy and complacency. It's not that this side of Jesus' Second Coming everything will be perfect, but it *is* that we should aim at nothing less, modelling on earth what only Jesus' return can do in fullness.

When Jesus lived and ministered on earth he found himself historically among people where there were four apparent practical options to the political situation and toward peace (I am grateful to Roger Forster for these ideas). The *Sadducees* were Israel's chief negotiators with the Romans. (Don't forget that at this time the Jews were oppressed and ruled by the Romans.) The Sadducees were despised as 'toadies', a compromised people, although the truth of the matter is that historically they had achieved some very useful bargains: the Jews alone of all Roman conquered nations did not have to provide male slaves to the Roman army, and they did not have to indulge in emperor worship. The Sadducees ingratiated themselves well with the Romans not least by levying various temple taxes and using the money thus raised to lend to the Roman administration and military. The Sadducees suffered from a lack of biblical perspective, however, in that they didn't believe in a physical resurrection or after-life (that's why they were Sadd-u-cee; sorry!).

On the other hand, the *Pharisees* had tried this form of political compromise manoeuvering under the leadership of Judas Maccabeus and had got their fingers badly burned. In Jesus time they had therefore become separatists, hypocritically using the advantages gained by the negotiations with the Sadducees, whilst warning against them. An outward observance of the law, politics and religion hid inward corruption in the Pharisees, who came in for the heaviest criticism from Jesus for those very reasons (see Matthew chapter 23).

On one extreme of these two factions was the third option: the *Zealots*. In the face of considerable oppression from the Romans, these Jews believed that God wanted his chosen people to be free (which is true), but they also believed that the ends justified the means and even sanctified the means, since they thought that God was pleased with those Zealots who killed most Romans! The idea was that might is right when might was Jewish. And so the Zealots were violent activists (Simon, one of Jesus' disciples [Lk 6:15], interestingly enough, had been a Zealot) who looked to force of arms to wrest power and political control from the privileged Romans and give it back to the oppressed Jews. Many Jews, while not being Zealots, believed the awaited Messiah would be a warrior king doing just that.

On the other extreme of the Sadducees and Pharisees lay the fourth political alternative in Jesus' day: the *Essenes*. They it was who left us the legacy of the Qu'mran texts—the Dead Sea Scrolls. John the Baptist had an Essene upbringing and reflected it in his style of ministry: seclusion and somewhat peculiar separatism. The Essenes judged the Sadducees compromisers, the Pharisees corrupt and the Zealots violent, and so they sought a place in the wilderness where they could build a good and perfect community and serve God's people Israel spiritually (hence the accuracy and preservation of the scripture portions we have from an Essene community) if not practically. Not only were the Essenes not of the world they were hardly even in it!

Jesus, however, knowing that the kingdom of God

was bigger than all of this, did not align himself with any of these positions. It seemed that Jesus Christ, as you might expect, was to find a radical fifth alternative. His response to world (Roman) domination, oppression and warfare, was a political one. (Politics allows the will of a group of people to reign, so God is therefore interested in politics, for he wants His own will to reign.) Jesus spoke of a kingdom: the kingdom of God would supersede the Roman kindom. Jesus died a political death. Paul spoke in political terms of an evangel, a good news, which heralded a new emperor or king. But this kingdom was a new sort of kingdom. The four old ideas outlined above are still around today in the Christian church and non-Christian society. Let me briefly outline what I believe are seven current misunderstandings about this fifth alternative, this kingdom which we're called to seek.

1. As the Roman empire collapsed, and Constantine made Christianity the state religion, power to reign went politically to the church. It therefore suited some church fathers (for example Augustine) to maintain that the church and the kingdom of God were one and the same, and so the parable of the wheat and tares started to be read (and still is) as meaning that the church is a place of redeemed and unredeemed together (see Mt 13:24–30). But the church can only consist of God's redeemed people: the parable of the wheat and the tares refers to the world not the church, where redeemed and unredeemed, saved and unsaved alike are affected by the kingdom (which is bigger than the church) and only sorted out in the end time of judgment. This wrong theology of 'the church equals the kingdom' led to hundreds of years of dark ages.

2. Reformation Protestant theology maintained that

the kingdom of God was God at work in the whole universe (which it is) but with God as a kind of grand master chess-player manipulating unresponsive chess pieces. There is an element of truth here as God is sovereign, but this limited view of kingdom overlooks two basic truths.

First, that Jesus himself became a 'chess piece' and chose to make his own moves through the encouragement he received from his Father. And secondly, that Jesus has given us back our humanity and dignity, and given us a new heart so that we can choose to do likewise. So the kingdom is expanded through dynamic interrelationship—that is, a friendship between God and his people, not through remotely dictated rules.

3. There is an idea (known as Hegelianism) that the kingdom of God is being formed through a kind of evolutionary process as we march ever onwards and upwards. This is really a sort of spiritualised humanism, a kingdom of man. It's a kind of religious Darwinism.

4. A popular idea today is that the kingdom of God is simply doing whatever God wants, thus evil men doing good are in and working for God's kingdom. But doing whatever God wants is actually our response to the kingdom of God and its claims on our actions; it doesn't constitute the kingdom itself. The kingdom can only be within those who have been redeemed.

5. Liberation theology, born in South America, is a direct crib from the early Jewish Zealots. It maintains that the kingdom of God is initiated by physical force against oppressors. The ends justify the means, and the kingdom is built through men's methods.

6. Fundamentalist evangelicals may divide the Bible

into various eras of God's dealing with humanity. Thus, for example, the gifts of the Holy Spirit could be consigned only to early church use, along with prophets and apostles. In much the same way, the kingdom of God can be consigned to a time only in the future, leaving us for the present only with the church. This is called Dispensationalism.

7. Finally, a growing misconception of the kingdom of God is that it is the structure of the church; the kingdom is the way one member of the body of Christ relates to another. This tends towards introversion, and apathy regarding the world.

In my opinion, these seven views are actually all wrong. The seeds for these ideas can be traced back to the four groupings prevalent in Jesus' time which is why I took the trouble to outline them. Without going into the implications too much, I'd like to offer a seven-point framework for the kingdom of God. Later we'll see how we can use this framework to arrive at a pattern of response to the nuclear threat. Remember, in this chapter all we're trying to do is establish a perspective on our reactions to the bomb and how it affects us all as Christians.

The kingdom of God is where God's will is done on earth against demons, sickness, sin and oppression (Mt 6:10) in the following way.

1. In the kingdom, prayer is centred on the workers not the harvest. The world is already ripe for the effects of the kingdom, but the workers (that is, the church) are largely unripe (Mt 9:35). Its with remembering that according to God 'judgment starts with the house of God' (1 Pet 4:17).

2. The kingdom goes to people who are aggressive (but not violent) in their faith (Mt 11:22).

3. The kingdom is marked by child-like trust (Mt 11:25; 19:14).

4. The kingdom net will encircle the world (not just the church), and then it will be gathered up and sorted out (Mt 13:47).

5. The power of Satan, his demons and his strategies (the city gates were where plans were formulated) won't stop the march of the church against them as we lead people to God who frees them from their bondage to sin (Mt 16:18).

6. The church is only twice mentioned in the context of the kingdom, and in Matthew 18:18 the reference is that the church has the keys to bind and loose activity on earth which will establish the kingdom of God. Our response to the nuclear threat involves much aggressive, faithful, persistent and fruitful prayer. But more of that in the last chapter.

7. The kingdom is advanced when we look our obstacles squarely in the eye. These obstacles may be in our personal life, our corporate life (the church) *and* the national and international scene. We must face the enemy (not flesh-and-blood Russians but the spiritual root behind people and circumstances) and by praying with faith in Christ's victory on the cross and in our lives, begin to disarm those enemies (Mt 21:21).

The overriding principle found in Matthew chapter 24 is simply this: until the kingdom comes in fullness, until Jesus returns and everyone submits to him, we must go for all that we can get of God's kingdom on the earth now.

Now, I know that the Bible gives balanced teaching about the end times. I know that as the light gets lighter so the dark gets darker. I know that as the kingdom of God expands (which it is currently doing more than at any other time in world history) so it pushes against the boundaries of the kingdom of Satan. I know that Jesus himself promised that things would go from bad to worse. But this does not give us an excuse for sitting back and simply watching. Look at it like this.

You're saved. You're forgiven. You are to be good news to the whole of society, as well as to individuals (in Acts 1:8 Jesus said be witnesses not just do witnessing). You are to extend the kingdom of God, not just build the church. Part of our redemption is to be stewards again of the creation that groans as it awaits Jesus' return (Rom 8:22). So what will your response be to nuclear threat and worsening world situations? 'Oh well, Jesus said it'll get worse anyway, so I might as well do nothing!' We don't carry on sinning just because we know God will forgive us. If we love him we will want to please him. In the same way, although the Bible warns us of the increasing dangers and evils of the end times, we should still work to lessen them. We mustn't disappear under a welter of fear or inactivity. We must hold in check all the tensions, balances and paradoxes that I've talked of in this chapter.

The world will be ravaged but it won't be annihilated. The world is God's despite Satan. The world is loaned to you and me as Christians. Salvation is for the individual but also has corporate implications for the church and society. God's kingdom is both here now in you and it's yet to come in Jesus. Things will get worse before they get better, but we are called to work while there is still light against cruelty, injustice, oppression, poverty and, in the case of this book, I believe against nuclear world threat (Jn 12:35–36).

All that remains is, in the following chapters, to work out just how we do it. We don't have the option on whether peace is a good thing or not; God is the God of peace and commands peacemakers (1 Cor 14:33 and Mt 5:9). Note that the word used is not peace*keepers*, for peace is an active force, not merely the absence or cessation of violence.

So far, we've examined a little of the history of the bomb, we've looked at the current world situation, and now in this chapter we've examined its effects on young people and tried to place that in a biblical framework against which we can check our basic response. But what are the biblical options? Can the bomb be a just defence? Is it a deterrent? How have Christians and non-Christians reacted to violence and warfare over the centuries, from the Old Testament onwards? Can the nuclear threat usefully provoke Christians to share more urgently the good news of a God of peace? Is there a biblical line on Christians and the bomb?

I believe that there is, and over the next few chapters we'll try to unpack it, and answer some of the questions.

4

Holy War?

'Don't talk to me about a God of love! How can you believe in a God of love when there's so much war and violence and bloodshed around? Religion has a chronic track record—you've only got to look at the Spanish Inquisition or Northern Ireland to see that. Look, either God's a God of love and he's very weak because it's not working, or he's not a God of love at all. Anyway, doesn't he command war and slaughter in the Old Testament?'

The spiky-haired, rather aggressive sixteen-year-old lad at a local sixth form college stuck his chin out and defied me, the world at large, and God, to satisfy him with an answer that made sense.

You must have heard the argument. You may have struggled with it yourself. Doesn't the Bible contradict itself in this whole area of war? Isn't the God of the Old Testament revealed as a war-inciting, nationalistic, vindictive being? Why is there such a contrast in the New Testament, where he is revealed as a God of mercy, grace and forgiveness whom we can call 'Daddy' (Rom 8:15).

Is God dead?

Even though the Third World War so far remains an unfulfilled threat, it can claim a major casualty: God. Many refuse to believe in a personal, loving, Creator when such a threat hangs over us all. Many people— among them many young people—argue that we, at the press of a button, have taken over the role of ruler of the world. One fifteen-year-old girl voices the doubt of her generation. 'How can you believe in God when the world is likely to get blown to pieces tomorrow or the day after?' (Quoted from *Family* magazine, January 1985.)

A recent survey at a comprehensive school of 600 eleven to fifteen year olds confirms this very common (and understandable) viewpoint. Thirty per cent believed a nuclear war was likely to happen in their lifetime, 21% thought that it would happen at any moment, and 91% didn't think they would survive any holocaust. Do the words of one twelve year old involved in the survey ring any bells with you? 'I think about the nuclear war every day. Like on a hot day when there are no clouds and the sky is blue, I think what a horrible thing if the nuclear war happened now...as to having children, in a way I would like to see new life springing up—but if the child was blown up what good would there be in having it?'

Child psychologists are increasingly recognising in their patients the curse of nihilism (the belief that there is no meaning or purpose to existence). And how can we refute the charge that the Bible, far from offering help, indicates from the Old Testament at least that God is a God of war?

The Old and New Testaments

The idea that the Old Testament contradicts the New Testament is not a new one. In the second century Marcion (circa 80–160 AD) taught that there were two Gods, the Jewish Creator-God of the Old Testament and a previously unknown God of the New Testament, Father of Jesus Christ. So we have a God of law and justice, and a God of mercy and salvation. He failed to recognise that law and justice meet mercy and salvation at one place and at one climactic time: the cross of Jesus Christ.

Most of the early church fathers rejected Marcion. However, in explaining how the God of Old Testament wrath could be the God of New Testament love, they decided that the Old Testament must be largely allegorical, not dealing with real wars or real massacres. But history, archeology and common sense tell us otherwise!

More modern thinking still struggles with the same problem. It usually either interprets the wars in the Old Testament as 'holy wars' in order to justify warfare today, or else writes off the Old Testament not as allegory, but as undeveloped in its revelation of God. The latter idea says that as mankind develops in understanding, so God develops the revelation of his character. So the primitive, war-like nation of Israel would only understand a primitive, war-like revelation of its God. This idea, however, takes no account of the unchanging nature of fallen people, nor does it take into account the Bible's own record of itself (for example 1 Tim 3:16) and of God (Jas 1:16–18).

So over the centuries we've had Constantine, in the fourth century, threatening his army with death or 'conversion' to Christianity. We've had the Crusades justified through texts like Jeremiah 48:10—when

Jerusalem was taken on the 15th July 1099, ten thousand Muslims were beheaded to please God! We've had the Inquisition in the thirteenth and sixteenth centuries. In 1718 the world saw James Puckle's gun with square bullets the better to kill infidels! We've had the religious facade justifying the slave trade in the nineteenth century, the subduing of nations for emperical expansion. And today we have the enforcement of apartheid and the turmoil of Northern Ireland. Countering colonialism with its 'justified' holy wars; we have the liberation theology of the 1960s where a politically and socially conscious church (a good thing) compromises its message of hope by taking up arms against the oppressors (a bad thing). Liberation theology has been largely a Latin American movement garnering some support from bodies like the World Council of churches. It is rooted in the Old Testament narratives of the Exodus and of warfare, and the element in the New Testament's teaching of the kingdom of God which describes Christians as exiles in this world. Yet it leaves out the very thing which it cannot afford to leave out—Jesus' teaching on how to deal with your enemies. For it is this teaching that spans the Old and New Testaments by linking in one man the holiness, justice and mercy of the God who is reflected in both Testaments. In this chapter I want to tackle one particular strand of the problem: the idea that God ordains 'holy wars', and that he actually promotes involvement in wars today that will advance his holy cause. This is different to saying that God allows wars as a last resort against a clear evil (this is called the 'just war' position, and we'll look at it in Chapter 6).

Disobedience breeds armies

In the Old Testament, God established the working of justice through men (Deut 1:15–17). He appointed judges to do this (2 Chron 19:6–7). Israel was governed by God in a unique 'theocracy' (that literally means 'God-government'), worked out through the Judges. It can be seen at work in the book of Judges in the Bible. This form of government was unique at that time (Lev 11:44; 20:23, Is 6:13) and has always remained unique. Although it worked well, the nation of Israel, looking around anxiously at their surrounding (and not always friendly) neighbours, began to want a king to lead them as they observed kings lead their neighbours. So, no longer content with *the* king and his Judges, Israel demanded a king, and God allowed them one. This first king, Saul, soon got it wrong (1 Sam 18), and David took over the role.

Now, it was with the arrival of the kings of Israel that Israel, no longer trusting in the direct government of God (theocracy) began to form an army—against the many clear warnings of the prophets (see Ps 20:7; Is 2:6–8; 31:1; Hos 10:13–15; Nahum 2:13; Zech 9:9–15, Mic 4:1–3. Please do look at these references, it makes the picture clear). So Israel's military might and potential was developed as the nation moved against God's rule, not with it.

This original outworking of justice was to maintain law and order, punish disobedience (Prov 17:15, Deut 16:8–13) and defend the poor and helpless (Prov 31:8–9, Ps 146:7–9). But it did include the death penalty (Deut 19:11–13) and also waging war. It is these last two areas that causes problems for Christian pacifists and for non-Christians who find it difficult to reconcile such an outworking of justice with a God of love. We can't shy away from such passages as Joshua 6:21,

Joshua 8:1–2, Joshua 10:40, Exodus 32:27, Judges
20:35, Judges 6:7, Deuteronomy 7:16, Deuteronomy
20:10–18, 1 Samuel 15:2–3, Psalm 149:6–9. Have a look
at them.

If holy wars are OK, why not...?

The problem here is that the Old Testament says too
much for those who would justify the waging of holy
war today. For the Old Testament is clear as to why
and how holy wars were fought then. In its descriptions
of great massacres it says too much for the modern
Christian seeking to validate a holy war. Should we
really today kill a whole nation? Should we have oblite-
rated Argentina in 1982 with a few nuclear bombs? Isn't
that more in keeping with an Old Testament holy war
than just sinking a few ships, downing a few planes and
killing and suffering losses of a relatively few soldiers?

Very few people who argue for a holy war would
push their argument that far, but if you were really to
have a holy war argument on the Old Testament basis
alone, you'd have to. Can we select which bit of the Old
Testament law and methods we keep, or should we live
in the better way of the New Testament?

If holy wars are OK, how come...?

Infuriatingly, the Old Testament also says too little to
satisfy those arguing for the validity of a modern-day
holy war. For the Old Testament is clear that on the
very few occasions when God commanded holy war, he
did so for very limited reasons and using very particular
supernatural means. The why and the how of Old
Testament wars says too little for the modern day pro-
ponent of such warfare. That is, it says trust God and

not military deterrent. So if you're going to argue, or meet other people who argue that war can continue today because it's in the Old Testament, then logically they must either argue that a holy war today means complete obliteration of whole nations (surely an unthinkable proposition in the light of the New Testament) or it means that we do without military might altogether and rely on God's supernatural intervention with his people. You see what I mean? The Old Testament says too much and too little to justify holy war.

The answers

Holy wars? Old versus New Testament? Is there any answer? I believe there is. The Bible is a united whole. You can't take parts of it out of context, and its apparent contradictions largely vanish when read as part of the whole. The Old Testament is a remarkable collection of thirty-nine books written by over forty different authors over more than 1,100 years, encompassing many styles. Despite tackling many deep and controversial subjects it is constant in its teaching, and in its revelation of mankind, and of God. The Old Testament is like a dictionary for the New Testament, giving us an understanding of words like sacrifice, covenant, atonement, redemption. The Old Testament is a driving force revealing God in human history, but always heading for the New Testament. We need to see both together; the light of the New Testament illuminates the Old Testament as well.

Prepare the way

As an escapologist if I am to present a new escape on stage, say from a water-filled padlocked drum, then I make very sure beforehand that I've prepared the way, set the scene for the audience, and checked that everything is ready. This is exactly what the Old Testament does for the New. In the Old Testament God provided a historical backdrop against which the coming of Jesus his Son would be expected, seen and recognised. Israel was chosen to reveal to the world the love of God, and to produce a solution to all the pain and evil of the world. It was from Israel that the seed of the Messiah would spring and bloom (Is 6). It's only when we see what a great purpose was at stake that we get a better context in which to understand the (sometimes) extreme lengths to which God went in the Old Testament to keep his people pure, focused on Himself, or even simply in existence. Lose Israel and the backdrop of prophecy, revelation of the Jewish God, and the need for and expectancy of a Messiah would all be lost too.

But is this an argument based on the ends justifying the means? When the end is the establishing of a means of salvation potentially for the whole world past, present and future, and when the person aiming at that end is no less than the perfect and just God, who can argue? And yet, it's not even as though God has said, 'I needed to have Israel wage war to keep them together and holy, to produce my Son to save the world.' Because if we examine the Old Testament itself, we'll see that even then, under extreme circumstances and provocation, God never simply brushed the means of his working aside. The wars in the Old Testament were very carefully embarked on and under such conditions as to be deliberately unrepeatable and unnecessary today.

Unrepeatable and unnecessary war

What does that mean? In the Old Testament, war didn't just happen at the whim of Israel (unless they were being disobedient), it happened *when* God clearly spoke, and it happened *how* he said it. War was not waged by military might but by God's direct intervention and prophetic word (have a quick look at Joshua 24:12, Exodus 15:1–18, Isaiah 5:6, 2 Kings 18:13–19:36, Judges 7:2–3, Deuteronomy 1:17, Exodus 28:30, Numbers 27:21, and so on). The means of warfare were miraculous and often directly supernatural (Deut 20:1–9, Joshua 11:6–9).

Old Testament Israel has no modern counterpart today. God still has much to say on her future as a nation, but there is no longer a holy nation by natural descent or geographical boundary, or one governed by theocracy. The New Testament has deliberately changed the focus. God's people are now a spiritual nation: Israel is the church; God's laws are written on our hearts by his Spirit; we are under the reign of his kingly grace and not law. There are deliberately no structures to allow us to fight, as though by God's command, against human enemies.

Difference not discrepancy

If there is no discrepancy between Old and New Testament in the character of God, we must be unafraid to see that there is a difference between the way he can work in Old and New Testaments. We must also realise that the Old Testament superseded by the New Testament precisely because the New Covenant is a better way.

The New Testament fulfills the Old Testament (it doesn't make nonsense of it; indeed, the Old Testament was important to Jesus both before and after his resurrection. Have a look at Luke 4 and Luke 24:27). Jesus said that it is a better way (Mt 5:22, 27, 33, 38 and 43). We should not underestimate how radically different was Jesus' teaching under the New Covenant, or how radically were the changes made to human nature at the time of jumping into the New Covenant (2 Cor 5:17).

The ultimate end behind war in the Old Testament was the person of Jesus Christ. He's already lived, died and been raised. The Church, the New Israel, can only bring in God's kingdom in his way. His way is spelled out in the Gospels, Acts and letters of the New Testament. It is a different and altogether better way to the Old Testament. The last two chapters of this book will try to spell out this better way.

Of course, suggesting that warfare is not only possible but even desired and commanded by God under the New Covenant, does not mean that the protaganists of the holy war view do not believe in God. The holy war position is therefore held by some Christians. It is also held by many religious people of other faiths. For example the Sikhs in the Punjab region of India with their militant defence of the Golden Temple, or the Shi'ite Muslims fighting the so-called Christian Militia, and the fanatical followers of the Ayotollah Khomenei to name but three. For some of these, to die in battle like the Vikings of old is to be a martyr and to ensure a greater certainty of access to 'paradise'. The Muslim version of the holy war, *Ji'had* (which means literally 'struggle'), is based on the commands of the Muslim scripture, the Qur'an. This demands that Muslims should 'fight in the way of God' against any opponents—though it also forbids the use of aggression.

But there is one other viewpoint besides the holy war

position that I would like to explore. This is not the concept of a holy war held by God-conscious people, but rather the concept of an 'unholy war', or non-Christian war, and the attempts which have sometimes been made to justify it. We will look at this in the next chapter.

5

Unholy War

It might be something of a surprise to discover that there are people (sometimes very powerful and influential people) who justify war from a purely humanistic perspective. If some Christians can argue a case for war based on God's commands and attitudes in the Old Testament (and call it holy war), then some non-Christians can argue a case for war based, like the First World War, on social, economic and political pressures (and I choose to call this unholy war).

Big business

When we consider that war is actually big business, it becomes obvious that many people will have a vested interest in perpetuating warfare. Every hour you spend at school or college, 42 million pounds is spent globally on arms. In the USA, there are 22,000 major corporations that exist for arms' manufacture, maintenance and sales. In 1976, ex-President Jimmy Carter, a self-confessed Christian, said, 'It is easier to talk about beating swords into ploughshares than it is to convert a

production line from jet fighters to subway cars…we
must face the reality that millions of Americans depend
on military spending for their livelihood…we must face
these problems squarely through intelligent and long
term conversion planning' (*New York Times* magazine).
He at least held out the possibility of an eventual shift
from military to civil investment of funds, but faced
then (as do today's world leaders) the fact that one
million dollars spend on defence in the USA in 1976
produced 75,000 jobs. That's a lot of votes per million
dollars!

Before we smugly condemn the situation across the
Atlantic, let's look at the plank in our own Islands! The
Ministry of Defence is one of the United Kingdom's
largest employers, with one million plus working for it.
Each year orders in excess of five million pounds are
placed with more than sixty UK contractors, and at
any given moment the Ministry of Defence has contracts out with more than 10,000 UK companies.

After the close of the 'war to end all wars', the First
World War, it was largely recognised that the con-
flagration had been primed, fired and fuelled largely by
economic motivations, even over and above political,
social or geographical circumstances. This led in the
United Kingdom in 1935 to a Royal Commission investigation on the arms' business. And this Commission
reported back that, in economic terms, 'the reasons for
maintaining the private industry outweigh those for its
abolition'. By the 1930s the United Kingdom was the
world's largest arms' exporter.

Though no longer the world leader, our investment
remains enormous. One-half of the British aerospace
industry and one-third of the British electronics industry is devoted to defence contracts, with things unlikely
to change in the foreseeable future as 54% of research

and development in the United Kingdom (for example, in telecommunications, robotics and biotechnology) is for military purposes. The big business of defence is not just restricted to those who make bombs and bullets; the investments of the associated industries are enormous.

Nuclear power—or bombs?

Take the nuclear power industry as an example. Now, you could be forgiven for thinking that because of government and British Nuclear Fuels Ltd advertising and promotional campaigns, that (a) we need nuclear power to generate sufficient electricity for our needs; (b) nuclear power is the cheapest, cleanest and safest form of energy available to us, and (c) the military usefullness of the results of nuclear power (for example, plutonium and uranium for warheads) was never derived from civil electricity producing plants, only from military plants, and was moreover a kind of incidental, almost accidental, by-product of making electricity.

But you would be wrong. None of (a), (b) or (c) is in fact true. By concentrating on nuclear fuel (which means investment of money in nuclear power) we have ignored other forms of producing natural energy, and of conserving the energy we currently use, as well as assessing more radically what we actually 'need'. What we need is a very relative term—one American uses twice as much commercial energy as one German, and all the fuel used by the Third World is only slightly more than the amount of petrol which the northern hemisphere uses in its cars (*The Brandt Report* 1980). Hence solar, wind and wave power are relegated to the place of fringe interests and portrayed as the intelligent but impractical pursuit of 'green' boffins. These alternatives need more funding and research, but all are cheaper, cleaner and safer than nuclear fuel, which currently only provides twelve per cent of our electricity anyway.

Nuclear power carries inherent risks of accident, pollution, difficulties of waste disposal, escalation of available bomb-making materials, misuse by terrorists and so on. As for which came first, nuclear power or nuclear weapons, and what continues to motivate our nuclear power programme, all we need do is look at the facts of history. After the Second World War, the nuclear collaboration between the USA and the United Kingdom broke down, and the United Kingdom began to forge its own way ahead. A nuclear fuel plant was built at Springfields near Preston in Lancashire, while uranium was to be enriched at Capenhurst near Chester. Meanwhile in February 1952, two military plutonium production reactors and a reprocessing plant were opened at Winscale in Cumbria. Materials suitable for making nuclear bombs were sent to Aldermaston, near Reading, and the United Kingdom successfully tested its first atom bomb off the North coast of Australia on 3rd October 1952.

After a disastrous nuclear accident (hushed up until the mid 1980s) in 1957, Winscale was closed down. But increasing military pressure had meant that in October 1956, Calder Hall, adjacent to Winscale was opened. In May 1959 Chapel Cross in Dumfrieshire was opened. For the *first* time, these two new plants were to produce electricity as well as nuclear fuel for military purposes. So it's bombs first and electricity second, then and now. For example, all plutonium produced in the UK (and therefore including that used in bombs) is reprocessed (made more efficient for exploding) at Sellafield—the

new 'clean' name for the old dirty Winscale! Some of
that plutonium used in making bombs comes from the
nearby nuclear power station at Calder Hall, and from
Chapel Cross. We have an assurance that nuclear fuel
from civil electricity plants isn't used to make bombs,
yet that is, in the words of a former Central Electricity
Generating Board Chairman (the late, much respected
Lord Hinton) 'bloody lies'. And 'Scientists Against
Nuclear Arms' research indictates that some two to
three tonnes of plutonium is unaccounted for in the
official figures. Lord Marsh has also gone on record as
stating that nuclear power development in the United
Kingdom is for the purpose of producing plutonium for
military purposes.

We can see from the above that the growth in arms
industries and defence research, and the destabilising of
a nation's economy that this may cause, are factors in
the promotion of unholy war. Military industries then
perpetuate such a war. Defence investment by industry
has saved giant employees (like Krupp in West Germany, Vickers in the UK, and Carnegie in the USA)
from annihilation. But defence investment hasn't saved
people from annihilation. Quite the reverse; annihilation (by bomb, bullet or cancer) has become big international business.

Economic alternatives

We have to decide if we're involved here in a case of 'if
it works it must be right' or 'the ends justify the means'.
Do we accept situation ethics: it's better to employ
people in defence than have them unemployed. Of even
worse, fatalistic humanism: someone would sell arms,
so we might as well do it and profit by it instead of
letting a fascist or communist government benefit? (The

same argument was used to propagate the slave trade.) Or *are* there absolutes involved? Does the Bible offer clear teaching and commands, and workable alternatives? The answer is Yes! I'd like to outline the conclusion I have come to, from my study of Scripture, in Chapter 8, but enough here to refute this economic concept of an unholy war by pointing out that realistic economic alternatives have never been properly tried because they've never been properly invested in.

There are economic alternatives to spending money on warfare and defence. Let me give an example. If 75,000 jobs could be created in 1976 by 1 million dollars spent on defence, it needs also to be pointed out that the same source (the United States Bureau of Labour Statistics) indicated that the same 1 million dollars spent on the construction industry would produce 100,000 jobs. In the consumer industry it would produce 112,000 jobs, in health 138,000 and in education 187,000 jobs—these last two categories are particularly important in our own country at the present.

Weapons or food

Is it morally right (let alone economically) to allow trade-offs on arms sales and sitings of armaments to become a lever of relationships between nations? We get on better with the USA diplomatically and economically because we use nuclear weapons sitings (for example, there were Cruise missiles at Greenham Common) as an economic tool. Is it morally right that 'developed' countries maintain power and economic dominance through military supremacy, and thereby force developing countries to plough their trading surplus (or more often their trading debts) not into agriculture, education or health, but instead into military expenditure? Is it morally right that globally we spend twenty-three times as much on arms per year than on development aid? A ten-year programme of essential food and health needs in developing countries is less than half of one year's military spending (*The Brandt Report* 1980). Globally we spend on arms in an hour what we in the United Kingdom gave to Ethiopia through Live Aid in 1985. And this isn't even taking into account the drain on research and development of health education and agricultural technicians that the military makes on more than half of our scientists, universities and industries. We're not far off the nightmare which George Orwell foresaw in his novel *1984* where Oceania was perpetually at war with either Eurasia or Estasia in order to maintain and preserve the economic and social balance and supremacy of Big Brother's Party. There must be a better way than all this!

Population explosion or explode the population?

But economics aren't the only factors put forward by the proponents of the unholy or non-Christian viewpoint on war. War has been proposed as the greatest and most efficient way of population control. That may sound absurd, but look at the way the world's population has been expanding, with all the attendant problems of famine, overcrowding, urbanisation, pollution, and so on. In around 6,000 BC the world population stood at about twenty million people, just twice the size of the population of greater London! After the time of the pharaohs in Egypt it surpassed 100 million. In Jesus' day it was around 150 million. Six centuries later it had doubled. The next doubling occurred 150 years after that. The next, 100 years later. By 1950 we were up to 2,500 million, 3,000 million by 1960, 4,000 million in 1980. Death control is outstripping birth control, and birth control in many countries is severely limited. Infant mortality rates are dropping. Eight and a quarter million people in the United Kingdom are below eighteen. Half of the population of Zimbabwe are under fifteen.

Faced with such an explosion of the world's population there are those who advocate decreasing the surplus population by propagating a different form of explosion! There is no doubt that the current economic and food situation worldwide would be far less stable than it is now, were it not for two world wars this century. War is a great exerciser of population control. And hidden away in the hills behind Hollywood, in the woods and plains in Kansas, in Sweden and in Switzerland, and even in Wiltshire, are survival bunkers stocked and readied by people who not only expect to survive a nuclear holocaust, but who spend much of their waking time dreaming and planning of the opportunities it might afford them to start civilisation again, to repopulate the earth but make a 'better' job of it their way. There is a whole industry of survival materials— books and provisions, etc—developing around such individuals. Their literature makes chilling reading. All this is before we even consider the Civil Defence programme. I know people in civil defence whose livelihood has depended on telling other folk that they should and can survive a nuclear holocaust, when all the statistics and estimates realistically show the horror of such a holocaust and the slim chance of surviving it (see Chapter 2). In the words of Long John Silver of *Treasure Island* fame: 'Them that die'll be the lucky ones!'

War might be viewed as a great reducer of surplus

population, but the fact of the matter is that despite
massive population increases, the earth is not as yet
remotely overpopulated. Localised famines and disas-
ters can be a result of a fallen world order because it's
not just people who fell but creation with them (Rom
8:18–25). They can equally be a result of the way fallen
man has failed to care for the earth. In Ethiopia (named
in the Bible as Cush) we are seeing the natural consequences of a nation which has worshipped other gods,
sacrificed children, been raped by a Marxist government and ravaged in agriculture as trees were ripped
down and sold to provide finance to buy guns for the
army. With tree loss goes a decrease in oxygen into the
atmosphere, which can lead to less rainfall and thus
drought. With tree loss goes soil erosion and thus loss of
land fertility. Much of this has happened in the last fifty
years or so.

The fact is that there is more than enough food to
feed the world many times over. The problem is, it's in
the wrong places. In the northern hemisphere we have
25% of the world's population and eighty per cent of its
income. The southern hemisphere has seventy-five per
cent of the world's population and twenty per cent of its
income. Life expectancy in the northern hemisphere
averages seventy plus years. In the southern hemisphere it's fifty years. Twenty per cent of the people in
the southern hemisphere suffer from hunger and mal-
nutrition; fifty per cent will never be literate. Ninety per
cent of the world's manufacturing industry is in the
northern hemisphere. India is now self-sufficient in
grain (twenty years ago it was like today's drought-and-
famine-ridden Africa) and even produces a slight surplus, yet sixty per cent of India's eight-hundred million
people are living below the poverty line (that is to say,

they do not earn the money needed to buy sufficient calories to sustain a normal life).

God's heart

What we need isn't a war to decrease the population; we need God's heart in the lives of activists in order to create a better redistribution of the wealth he's provided in this world. Then we will be reflecting his attitudes and his bias to the poor (Lk 1:51–53; Is 61:1). God has plenty to say about the solutions to famine, drought and 'apparent' overpopulation. He set the laws of Jubilee (Leviticus chapters 5 to 10 and 27:34) where every fifty years all debts were cancelled, all oppression lifted, all slaves set free, and all land redistributed. God is against the private accumulation of the much by the few at the expense of the many. God does bless us with success and prosperity so that we can fulfil Jesus' recorded statement that 'It is better to give than to receive'—one of the few sayings of Jesus which is not put down directly, but is important enough to record indirectly in the Acts of the Apostles (Acts 20:35). Jesus declared that in his own lifetime he was fulfilling the Jubilee (have a look at Luke 4:18–19 and compare it with Isaiah 61:1).

God has much to say on our treatment of 'foreigners', and it's not to drop bombs on them and so reduce the surplus population. Have a look at Leviticus 19:34 and Deuteronomy 10:19. The poor, orphans and widows are included for special care and attention (see Ex 22:22; Deut 24:17; Prov 23:10–11; Jer 7:6). And God hasn't changed from Old to New Testament, as we saw in the last chapter. Rather, he's fulfilled the Old Testament in a new and better way through Jesus Christ.

War as a safety valve?

There is also a theory that war is not only an inevitable product of human nature in its constant quest to acquire, dominate and establish territory, but that war is a desirable 'safety valve' to mankind's inherent aggression. The idea is that we have a kind of sub-conscious aggression muscle which needs the occasional flexing if it isn't to go into spasm. Therefore the constant national and international acts of aggression around the world, the seventeen or so wars currently going on worldwide, are all evidences of the necessary flexing of this aggression muscle. And moreover, if such 'mini-wars' weren't happening, we'd be in imminent danger of a major muscle spasm, which is what the First and Second World Wars were alleged to be.

The Falklands' crisis (it was never eventually declared as a war) in 1982 goes some way to validate such a theory—great nationalistic fervour over a conflict sufficiently far away and relatively unimportant to the welfare of the United Kingdom to enable the nation to flex its 'aggression muscle' without incurring too much personal danger! It was war by TV, and made stars of its own Ministry of Defence spokesman. All very well for armchair soldiers.

Of course, if this theory is correct then we are on a global scale well overdue a cataclysmic 'spasm'. It is now some forty years since the last 'spasm' which was in turn only twenty-one years after the world declared that such a catastrophe as World War I must never be allowed to occur again. Could it be that nuclear weapons are heightening not only fear and tension, but also the possibility of sudden 'aggression muscle' spasm rather than keeping the peace in Europe, as the USA and the governments of NATO countries claim? Are 'small' wars to be welcomed as a safety valve? Some would say so.

Territorial expansionism

Some would argue (either nostalgically looking back-wards or wistfully dreaming into the future) that nationalistic expansion is a valid reason for an unholy war to be waged. This 'Empire thinking' pushed the 'thin red line' of the British troops all around the world at the close of the last century. Large elements of the same thinking were evident in the Falklands' crisis, though of course those islands are solely inhabited by (Argentina would say 'occupied by') UK citizens. On 3rd July 1982, Mrs Thatcher was quoted as saying that people were disproved who thought that 'Britain was no longer a nation that had built an Empire and ruled a quarter of the world.' She went on to say, 'Well they were wrong. The lesson of the Falklands is that Britain has not changed.'

Is that all we learned from the Falklands? And what a terrible thing to learn! Colonial expansion alive and well in Britain.

The same thoughts of expansionism were behind the Third Reich in the Germany of the 1930s and 1940s. You can see it in Russia's occupation of Hungary, Czechoslovakia, Poland and Afghanistan. In the United Kingdom in Northern Ireland. And in the IRA blowing up British soldiers. It's based on attitudes of pride, domination, and the illogical ability to relegate some ethnic groups (like Jews, blacks, homosexuals, Protestants or Catholics) as being 'inferior' to others.

Full employment and community spirit?

I've even heard it argued that a good reason for war is that it will provide full employment. It's the kind of 'thinking' betrayed by comments like 'three years in the army would do them all good!' Of course, in the event of a nuclear war, there wouldn't be time for full employment.

And finally, you must have come across the attempt to justify or excuse war in terms of its ability to create the kind of cameraderie that exists between people in the same fix. Many older people will tell you of the openness and friendliness of folk united behind a common cause during the Second World War. Or look at the portrayal of strength that comes through adversity in any film about a disaster. Now, there is obviously *some* truth in this, albeit good brought out of bad, but with the distancing of time comes a rather rosier glow to history than facts would indicate.

It's the patina of age. After all, nostalgia's not what it used to be! The human mind has an amazing ability to forget pain, fear and anxiety quite quickly, while remembering good aspects of the same incidents. I'd rather see people united behind the love and peace of Jesus Christ than behind a war cause. I'd rather see people united behind the cross of Christ than behind an SS20 nuclear missile. And I'd rather see people united behind the empty tomb of the risen Jesus Christ than behind an abandoned Cruise missile base, even if it is in the United Kingdom.

I have tried to do justice to the 'non-Christian' arguments for what I term an 'unholy war', but it's very difficult. They are arguments used by politicians, economists, sociologists and military strategists, as well as by easily manipulated 'popular opinion.' But measured against the evil, the horror and the human cost of warfare, and as we'll see later, against God's own workable absolutes on violence, they are non-arguments. Even logically, let alone morally, you'd have to be more concerned with statistics on paper than with people to propagate such insanities in the first place. Most politicians seem to use statistics in the way that drunks use lamp posts—that is, for support rather than illumination! We must resist the urge to do likewise.

6

Can War Be Just?

You may not be familiar with the thinking behind the theory of 'just war,' but it has been the bedrock of popular Christian response to the whole problem of war for the last 1,600 years. There is such a great weight of tradition and practice behind it, that the chances are you will adhere to the underlying views of the just war even if you've never seen them set down before. And if you don't, you will certainly know (and probably argue with) people who do. So lets check it out!

At its simplest, the notion of a just war is that in certain circumstances it becomes necessary and inevitable to wage war. It's the idea that, while war is never good, it may sometimes be the lesser of two evils, where the greater evil would be loss of freedom, persecution, injustice and oppression, or man's slaughter. So in the Second World War it would be argued that the United Kingdom's stand against Hitler's Germany was necessary to destroy the evil of the third Reich's murderous fascism. Or that the Cold War between the USSR and the USA could rightly escalate into a nuclear war, because it's necessary to preserve democracy against communism, free enterprise against fixed monopolies, freedom of religion against an atheistic state, etc.

Those sincere and thinking Christians who hold to the just war stance do so not to encourage and 'justify' war but rather to try to limit warfare to a minimum. They do this by establishing certain quite rigorous criteria by which war can take place. If these criteria are not met, then war would be morally wrong. Most Christians evaluate their decisions by 'feel' or 'expedience' (ie 'do I think this will work? Is there an alternative') as I did before researching this subject. It's important to examine the foundations of the just war view before we build a case for nuclear weapons and possible warfare based upon the just war situation. Because if the foundations don't hold, then the whole argument may be in danger of collapse.

The historical background

First, a word or two about history. The just war tradition has its roots in the holy wars of the Old Testament. The just war tradition also takes some of its moral stances from Greek and Roman ethics, both military and philosophical. These ideas were 'Christianised' in the fourth century by Augustine of Hippo (AD 354–430), by Ambrose and by Aristotle I, at least partially because of political developments. The Emperor Constantine had embraced Christianity and was determined that his army should do likewise; in AD 313 he baptised his troops and for the first time Christianity and the State because officially linked. It was the end of the persecution of the Christian church which began with its birth in Jerusalem. When politics made warfare expedient, theology now had to find a means of monitoring and morally limiting such warfare, and so the just war theory began to be expounded. The ideas were systemised by the theologian Thomas Aquinas in the thirteenth century and were further developed in the sixteenth century by the theologian Fransisco de Vitoria. Today these ideas (which are really an overlap of several viewpoints over the centuries) remain the most commonly held Christian viewpoint on warfare, including *nuclear* warfare.

Throughout the development of the just war theory, a number of consistent criteria have been used to determine the 'rightness' of the cause, the extent of the force used, and against whom it was waged. Seven has always been a good biblical number, so here are the seven criteria used to assess a just war.

1. The war should only be waged as a last resort, all other avenues (political, diplomatic, economic, spiritual, etc) having been explored (see Deut 20:12).

2. The cause of the war should be clearly just; the fight must be against a clearly recognised evil and against oppression (Ex 21:24).

3. The war should be begun and continued with right attitudes inspired by restraint and justice which can lead to possible reform and repentance, and *not* inspired merely by desires for retribution.

4. The war should be preceded by a declaration of intent, which can serve as a warning and opportunity for the enemy to back down. It should be begun only by a legitimate authority and not by disgruntled citizens with self-appointed powers.

5. There must be a reasonable chance of success where the cost of war (in terms of lives, property, political instability, etc) is outweighed by the ultimate good

results (eg, freedom from injustice and oppression).
Otherwise the end wouldn't justify the means.

6. There should be non-combatant immunity as stated
in Article 48 of the Geneva Convention. This immunity
of civilians must be proportional to the majority killed
or injured. It is accepted that non-combatants will of
course always be killed in war but this should not be by
intent by rather as an acceptably low by-product of
targeting combatants (eg the armies). This by-product
of dead civilians in modern warfare is called 'double
effect'. Some would argue that in modern warfare there
are no non-combatants because taxation from civilians
helps pay for government war machines, and also
because of the many ways in which civilians' services
would be used to support the war effort, for example, on
the areas of technology and medicine. So some proponents of the just war theory would remove this sixth
criteria. But even allowing for this, what of the non-tax
payers? What of the sick and the elderly? Under no
circumstances can they be termed combatants. Nowadays with 70 million Christians in the USSR and 50
million in China, Christians on one side would inevit-
ably end up killing Christian non-combatants on
another. In the Old Testament, total annihilation was
always reserved for total guilt (see Gen 6:5; 18:32; Lev
18:25). Judgment, at God's specific command, is pro-
portionate to the evil, and so at times in the Old Testament, the solidarity of an evil nation overrules the
principle of non-combatant immunity. Just war proponents argue (from an understanding of Romans chapter
13) that retribution, punishment and death come from
God's delegated authority to human governments. It's
worth reading through Romans chapter 13 at this point,
though we will look at it in more depth elsewhere in the
book. Notice that in Romans chapter 13 it is the legal

systems of weighty and careful consideration which give rise to the decision of who is guilty and who is 'innocoent'. The just war theory relies upon the ability to differentiate between the guilty and the innocent and so wholesale slaughter has to be ruled out. So there must be non-combatant immunity.

7. The good results of the warfare should outweigh its evils: not only the idea of success (see point 5), but also the idea of keeping a sense of proportion of the cost. This is success not at any price, but success which contains enough of the way of life which is being fought over in order to make the fight worth while. No Pyrrhic victories allowed!

Now since the fourth century all just wars have, in theory, had to comply with these seven standards in order to be called 'just' at all. A little later in this chapter I'd like to assess whether in fact this tradition is valid morally and biblically, but for now let's assess these criteria from the perspective of our age of the bomb. In other words, by its own criteria, can a nuclear war ever be called a 'just war'?

If it should come to a nuclear war there are three main options open to the strategists: 1. All-out nuclear war; 2. Limited-attack nuclear war; 3. Military-defined targeted attack on the enemy's forces.

Let's examine each and see if any qualify as a just war under that theory's own criteria outlined above. Bear in mind that these seven criteria merely say in longer words what most folk (Christian and non-Christian) feel by common sense (we'll look later at whether that common sense is biblically workable).

1. All-out nuclear war

This approach to war satisfies the first two criteria; it would never be (deliberately) undertaken except as a last resort because it's too risky. And there may be just cause to restrict the spread of the USSR's harsh, inhuman and unjust influence in Hungary, Czechoslovakia, and Afghanistan, though always remembering that the USA or United Kingdom are not God's own country either. But the question is at what cost?

Certainly all-out nuclear war does not have justice rather than retribution as its aims. Wanton and repeated strike-by-strike destruction of population centres is nothing other than pointless blow-for-blow vengeance, with no one the winner and the world the loser. In a nuclear war there would be no neutral countries which would escape damage, because radioactive fallout is no respecter of frontiers or treaties. Nor is the twenty-four minutes it takes missiles to reach Moscow from Washington, or vice-versa, a suitable time of warning or declaration of intent enabling any government machinery to back down. There can be no chance, let alone reasonable chance of success in the event of an all-out nuclear war with estimates of 190 million dead in the States and 160 million dead in Russia and with all the fallout effects on health, supplies, food, climate.

An all-out nuclear war deliberately targets non-combatants rather than seeking to give them immunity. The aim is to devastate entire countries and massacre their populations. And finally, what good results would outweigh unleashing enough destructive power to destroy the world? The question wouldn't be is there good left? The question would be is there anything left?

2. The threat of limited-attack nuclear war

Here the idea is that one Russian city wiped out would lead to one American city destroyed and so on. This is no more justifiable than all out nuclear war; it's just rather less effective in its destructiveness. If it's wrong to abuse 1 child sexually, then it's wrong to abuse 500. If it's wrong to sexually abuse 500, then it's wrong to abuse 1. If it's wrong to drop a nuclear bomb on 500 cities by the just war's own criteria, then it's wrong to drop a nuclear bomb on 2 cities. There may be more chance of 'success'—there may however be more chance of escalation to an all out nuclear war. Either way, limited-attack nuclear warfare does not provide for non-combatant immunity either, and has as its motive vengeance.

3. Military-defined, targeted attack

This is a relatively new feature in the scenario of nuclear war. Previously the superpowers existed uncomfortably under the threat of Mutually Assured Destruction. This is the idea of 'You hit me and I'll annihilate you!' But since the 1960s and 1970s, with the advance of technology, it has been suggested that nuclear war could be fought on a limited strategic front, targeting military bases only, or at least primarily. President Carter's Presidential Order No 59 confirmed this, and the accuracy of Cruise missiles and MX missiles and a smaller yield of enhanced radiation weapons (the neutron bomb) make such military targeting all the more viable.

But would there really be a reasonable chance of success? Is it likely that such a war could be confined to military targets? Human nature and the lessons of history indicate not. The law of diminishing returns

presses human nature to move from one military target
to a bigger military target and then to what? Civilian
targets? Once use a nuclear bomb, however small or
localised, you've removed the 'fire break' between the
horrors of conventional weapons and the totally anni-
hilistic nightmares of nuclear warfare. For example, in
the Second World War the United Kingdom deplored
the German air-raids against cities such as Liverpool
and Coventry. Churchill and Roosevelt vowed not to
use such methods. Yet as the Second World War escal-
ated, so-called saturation bombing on Hamburg in
1942–43 on Dresden in 1945, on Cologne and on Berlin
killed thousands upon thousands: in two days in Dresden about 135,000 people were killed. And then at the
end of the war there was Hiroshima. And then
Nagasaki. And so we see the horrors of escalation. Is it
likely to be different with military-defined, targeted
attack?

But it's not only human nature which indicates that
a nuclear war fought on military targets would not
remain there. With the increase in nuclear weapons
comes the possible increase in accidents, either through
human or mechanical, electrical faults. We've already
suggested that electromagnetic storms caused by limited nuclear explosions would render many electrical
systems inoperative or faulty. So what would happen to
a guided system, or a computer fail-safe system, or a
submarine to headquarters communication link during
the course of what might have begun as a limited
nuclear war against military targets only? How long
before panic through loss of communications, or before
computers accidently tripping missile silos would cause
such a limited warfare to escalate to allout attack?

In any case even military non-combatant nuclear
warfare (called limited counterforce strategy) has hor-

rendous implications for civilians even though they're not the primary target. For example twenty such military bases are targets in Moscow alone! Estimates indicate that such a limited war would immediately kill twenty million people in the USA and a slightly lower number, because of less dense population, in the USSR. There is no way that this can be described as proportional non-combatant immunity as required by one of the criteria of the just war concept. This is mass destruction of millions of civilians.

We've already seen in a previous chapter that military attack with the possibility of wiping out all land-based missile silos might make a first strike successful and in that case more likely. And if first strike is more likely than so is 'launch on warning' alone more likely. So the chances of warfare are increased and not decreased by the possibility of military attack alone.

So there are three options open to strategists for nuclear warfare; all-out, limited, or military attack. And none of those three meets the criteria of the just war for reasons explained above. But in my view there is a much deeper objection, and it is simply this: that despite tradition, the just war theory itself is wrong, both in practical terms and according to the Bible.

Let's check it out. Think back to its history. The theory of just war was developed to validate (and at best limit) the wars which the Emperor of the (now) 'Holy' Roman Empire waged on his opponents. Constantine had for the first time made conversions 'compulsory' to the extent that he would only have 'Christians' in his army. Church and state were wedded, and both headed for the Dark Ages. Yet previous to this, the Christian church had for 300 years been consistently anti-war. In those 300 years we have the recorded testimonies of only eight Christian soldiers. In

AD 170, the pagan author Celsus had written that there would be no army at all if everybody were Christians! In AD 197 the early church father Tertullian wrote to rebuke Christians who were still soldiers. By the third century church writings called the Canons of Hippolytus allowed that Christians in the army could 'police' civil laws but they were not allowed to kill.

It is sometimes argued that the reason why early Christians were encouraged to leave the army was not because of the need to take up the position of a pacifist but because the Roman army practised idolatry in the form of emperor worship. And yet it was only the officers of the Roman armies who were commanded to sacrifice, and Christians were allowed to stay in the army with the command not to kill rather than with the command not to sacrifice which would have been taken for granted anyway. The issue here therefore seems to have been one of war and not peace, of killing and of not forgiving. It was not an issue of idolatry. As the church father Origen (AD 183–254) said, 'We Christians no longer take up the sword against nation, nor do we learn to make war any more, having become children of peace for the sake of Jesus…who is our Commander.' These early church fathers were not the exception. The writings of many others reflect that in its first 300 years, the church was pacifist in thought and deed.

If we must look to tradition, I'd prefer to look at those founders of the Christian Church who were that much nearer the Founder in time, and who reflected rather than changed the, then, current practices of the early Christians. It also needs to be said that just war cannot be condoned because of the potential slaughter of Christians by Christians. Should the USA and Europe destroy the USSR, then we would be annihilating 70 million Christians. What of the Bible's teaching on the unity of the body of Jesus Christ whatever our race (1 Cor 12:13)? And what of Paul's teaching on our united rejoicing or suffering (1 Cor 12:26)? How can we with one hand support the Jubilee Campaign or Open Doors Ministries to the persecuted Church and with the other condone potential mass destruction?

Some people argue that if justice is allowed and necessary *within* a state—for example, justice as exercised by the police or the judiciary (see Romans chapter 13), then international justice across states must mean the possibility of war. I do not believe justice ever means war, but it's important to remember that in a state there is a separate neutral mechanism which can coolly investigate the 'justness' of a case. In war, not only is there no such cool approach, but there is as yet no separate global arbiter, so each nation becomes not only judge and jury but also potential executioner. And more yet: in the event of nuclear war, there will probably be no time to judge issues rationally.

Actually, the seven criteria of a just war have never been satisfactorily weighed or even met. The fact that they exist does make us think about what is or is not a fair cause for fighting. But the deeper question is: 'Is there ever a just reason for killing your enemy?' Even in the Second World War, an apparently clear case of a just cause, there were Christians on both sides, supporting both régimes and both claiming 'God with us'. In my opinion the just war position is untenable. Limited violence is, I believe, less realistic than non-violence. And never more so than in the nuclear age at the beginning of which Einstein said, 'The unleashed power of the atom has changed everything save our modes of thinking and thus we are drifting towards unparalleled catastrophe.' The old just war concept is now impractical. Not only that, but it is increasingly easy to see its moral gaps. Founded on tradition as it was (rather than biblical truth and absolutes), these moral gaps have always been there.

Every development within warfare has at first been condemned by the Christian Church, then eventually accepted and condoned under the system of just warfare where the ends justify the means. It happened with the crossbow which was banned at the Second Lateran Council in 1139; it happened with seige machines, then with gunpowder. With the revolver. With the machine gun—an early precurser, the Puckle gun of 1718, even had square bullets to shoot infidels and round ones to shoot Christians! It happened with the aeroplane, and now nuclear weapons. We have 20 megaton bombs which can now attain a temperature of 18 million degrees farenheit or eight times that of the heat of our sun's centre. We have between 50 and 60 thousand nuclear weapons. Ever since Cain we have learned to kill in pursuit of our own (personal or national) interests.

Is there a workable alternative? If so, when will we learn it? Will the futility of possible nuclear holocaust become, through God's grace and his people (Rom 8:26), redemptive? That is, will it turn us to look for a better way? Einstein said that 'A new type of thinking is essential if mankind is to survive.' It is my believe that a New Testament type of thinking fits the bill.

7

Can't Use, Can't Threaten?

It seems to me that anyone who examines the various arguments for and against the use and control of nuclear weapons has one major argument left to struggle with, which doesn't fall into the category of holy war, just war, or non-Christian war. It's perhaps the single most prevalent argument used to justify the stockpiling, servicing and development of nuclear arms. It's the last 'wall' in the nuclear silo I'd like to attempt to push over before we look at the biblical teaching on war, and on the practical alternatives for providing peace. This last argument is the one which sees the bomb as deterrent.

Deterrence is based on an attempt to make the best of a bad scene. In a letter to a friend of mine from the Defence Arms Control Unit of the Ministry of Defence, the following explanation of deterrence was proferred:

> In an imperfect world political responsibility often means choosing the least of several evils...the essential issue is whether it's morally right to possess nuclear weapons in order to prevent others attacking or threatening to attack

us. The greater good is undoubtedly served by preventing war.

Now, no one in their right mind would want to disagree with that last sentence. But it does raise the following questions: whether deterrence works to prevent war, whether choosing a 'lesser' evil is morally right, and whether possessing nuclear weapons is actually evil.

The reasoning behind deterrence is older than the nuclear debate and has been used in many situations of threat in the world. It has also had some forty years of application to our nuclear age. The thinking is fairly complex and deserves careful, prayerful study. The supporters of deterrence would say that their views are based on the following arguments.

1. Realism

We live in a fallen and imperfect world. Not all individuals, let alone states and governments, are like-minded, and many are certainly not Christ-minded. Hence the eloquent statements from Dean Inge: 'It is useless for the sheep to pass resolutions in favour of vegetarianism when the wolf remains of a different opinion.' Or Lord Carrington's address to the Royal Institute of International Affairs, Brussels, in October 1984:

> No householder could assume from the fact that he had not been burgled while in the house that there would be no risk of burglary if he left it empty. It is no more sensible to assume that the Soviet Union would behave, in a situation where it had a nuclear monopoly, as it had behaved in a situation where it knows itself to be vulnerable to devastating nuclear retaliation. The sensible conclusion in both cases is to keep the insurance policy up to date.

The rhetoric is good, the picture is vivid. But aren't there fundamental differences between the images used and the real situation? Insurance policies also cover you for accident. And if the worst comes to the worst and you are burgled, you still have a house—and a life. But what if the cost of the premiums means that you and your family can't care properly for your health and education? What if the cost of the premiums for the international economy means that ultimately a family in the Third World can't afford to buy food? What's the priority then? Perhaps Dean Inge's punchy picture should be contrasted with the words of a much more influential man: 'Listen! I am sending you out just like sheep to a pack of wolves. You must be as cautious as snakes and as gentle as doves' (Mt 10:16). Who would you rather follow?

Yet the argument based on realism is a strong one. It maintains that Jesus' teachings and the general morality of love can only apply to individuals and not to states. It argues that if the individual can accept the personal and national deterrent nature of a police force, then why not accept on the international scene the deterrent nature of nuclear bombs? It says that the 'peace' we now 'enjoy' is so fragile because of our fallenness. It's suggested that realism played its part in the heavy Labour defeat of the 1983 general election when Labour adopted a unilaterist position in its manifesto, something which it has since dropped.

2. A lesser evil

It is also suggested that deterrence works because it is less evil to threaten to use nuclear warheads than it is to surrender to oppressive, destructive atheistic forces. Anyone who suggests that nuclear weapons should be abandoned can be acused of sacrificing the moral values of freedom and justice to the god of survival. It is pointed out that for the Christian, survival is not the only moral consideration, but that quality of life is also vital. Unilaterists are therefore accused of the extreme position 'better red than dead'. And of course, deterrent supporters are often branded by the dictum 'better dead than red'. But it's not that simple either way.

3. No war in Europe

There has been no major war in Europe in the last four decades, so some people say that proves that deterrence works. Nuclear weapons, far from causing war or heightening its likelihood, have deterred such a war. So the argument goes.

4. No alternatives

The case for deterrence seems completed by the lack of any alternatives. Nuclear weapons can't be disinvented. If all stockpiles were removed this year, and then next year war broke out, there is no guarantee that, given human nature, someone wouldn't rebuild them and then use or threaten to use them. They could be dismantled (as per the Reagan/Gorbachov agreement on medium-range strategic missiles), but even then verification to check that they've been dismantled is needed, and not just that they've been redistributed or rearranged (as has happened already under the Reagan/Gorbachov agreement, with some nuclear warheads previously targeted on the USA now being switched to point towards Europe!). But dismantling even when properly done, isn't disinventing. There do not seem to be any viable alternatives, hence the Ministry of Defence's letter to my friend stating that 'there is therefore a moral duty not to abandone [a deterrence policy] except for one which makes the risk of war even less'. Fair enough. But is there such an alternative?

Deterrence and Christian morality

As Christians, before we can look for alternatives we have an additional set of arguments we dare not leave unconsidered. We have to find out what the Bible says about the deterrence argument, not just what is expedient. There are a few intriguing arguments from a Christian perspective in favour of deterrents which, added to the four above, make a formidable case for the bomb as deterrent. Let's have a look at these added 'pros' before we look at the 'cons'.

1. Authority

Christians in favour of deterrents have argued that since authority is given by God and should be obeyed (Rom 13), then the same applies internationally. A police force in the United Kingdom—an army on the Rhine. A truncheon in the town is worth a nuclear bomb in NATO. If we accept law and order and not anarchy nationally through the deterrence of the police force, then we should morally (not merely realistically) accept law and order and not anarchy internationally through the deterrence of the nuclear bomb and armed forces.

In fact, there's an interesting extension of this moral argument for deterrence. Some Christians would go on to say that God, being a redemptive God, takes the products of the Fall and makes them work for good. As the Apostle Paul says, 'We know that in all things God works for good with those who love Him, those whom He has called according to His purpose' (Rom 8:28). So the line of thinking continues that the state, national-ism, governments, etc, are both a result of (Gen 11:1–8) and a partial remedy for the Fall. Without the Fall there would have been no disunity between groups of people and no need for war or threats of war.

But since the Fall, God has chosen to use the very products of the Fall to save us from ourselves, hence his investment in governments (Rom 13, 1 Pet 2:11–17) and his approval of the bomb kept as deterrent. He takes weapons of horrendous, indiscriminate mass destruc-tion of people and plant, and brings good out of them by ensuring that, through a policy of deterrence, they'll never be used. So the argument goes.

2. From nuclear non-use to conventional non-use

Another aspect of the Christian pro-deterrence stance is the idea that deterrence will incline governments more toward conventional weapons than nuclear ones. The theory is that deterrence only works because both sides know that if the weapons are used it will be at enormous cost to everyone. Because the cost is so unthinkable deterrence should provoke a switch to developing more and more conventional weapons which we would con-sider using, and the more likely we are to use these weapons if pushed, the greater the deterrence.

3. 'Just deterrence'

Christians also point out that deterrence aligns itself closely with that most prevalent Christian attitude con-cerning war—the 'just war' theory (see Chapter 6). The idea is that it is morally defensible to have a specific minimum force adequate to determine any potential aggressor, especially when used to gain pro-gressive disarmament. This is a kind of 'just deter-rence'.

It is on these bases that Christians will often look at what the various denominations say and quote them to show an agreement that deterrence is biblically, morally and practically acceptable. The Pope, in June 1982, said that 'Deterrence…as a step towards progressive disarmament, may be judged morally acceptable'. Roman Catholic Bishops in the USA and Germany agreed with this, but added a further qualification: 'We cannot consider such a policy as a long term basis for peace.' They contradicted the famous statement of the Roman General, Vegetius, who said, 'If you wish for peace, prepare for war,' by saying rightly, 'If you wish for peace, defend life.'

The Church of England's General Synod, in February 1983 and again in 1989, was more rigorous and direct in proposing this 'just deterrence' idea: 'It is the duty of Her Majesty's government and her allies to maintain adequate force to guard against nuclear blackmail.' 'Adequate' was defined as a minimum deterrence, and not therefore necessarily equal with the force of the enemy. Unilateralism was defeated in the Church of England's General Synod by a three-to-one majority in 1983.

Then again, didn't Jesus say in the end times that there would be wars and rumours of wars? (Mt 24:3–14). Who are we as Christians to work actively against this? We might even find ourselves working against God's plans to end the world—the final Armageddon.

John Stott, in his book *Issues Facing Christians Today* makes a very good defence of deterrence as a necessary and moral interim while aiming at multilateral disarmament. He argues that because using the bomb as deterrent means that the intention behind the possession of nuclear weapons is not to use them, then it's not immoral to possess nuclear weapons. The motivation and thinking behind possession are what matters here, and by intending not to use them, John Stott maintains that biblically and morally we can keep on the right side of a passage such as Matthew 5:27–30, which also deals with motive and attitude rather than sinful temptations—have a quick look at it.

Do your own dirty work!

The Christian who argues for deterrence clearly and rightly points out that it would be immoral for the United Kingdom to reject nuclear weapons as a means of defence and deterrence, while still accepting NATO's protection and that of the USA, whose programmes include nuclear weapons. That would be like condemning hanging because you didn't like it and couldn't do it, but happily letting someone else do it for you. If dirty work must be considered as a possible, if necessary, option, then morally we must be prepared to do our own dirty work and not benefit from someone else's!

So there it is: a positive armoury of rational practical, moral and Christian arguments for deterrence. Can they be refuted? If so, we must look for nothing less than a rational, practical, moral, Christian absolute and alternative. For the bomb as deterrent doesn't look to justify war if it happens (just war), nor to condone war anyway (non-Christian unholy war), nor to see war as a kind of God-inspired crusade (holy war). Rather it aims to prevent war totally. We must do justice to this position. It's the fundamental basis for the current world situation between the superpowers, the Nuclear six. It's the framework of NATO's policy for the United Kingdom.

I'd like to try and point out what I see as really major practical and moral flaws in the deterrence position, and hope in the course of the next few paragraphs to refute the arguments that I've taken care to explain above. You must decide for yourself what you think not just on the basis of how well I marshall my arguments, but also on the Bible's revelation of God's character, human nature, on what he says to you, and on common sense.

Countering the argument for deterrence

We must be very clear about the building-blocks that go to make up the deterrence argument. Deterrence only works on the basis of both sides (or all sides, to make it more complicated) having too many weapons to destroy in a first strike, so that no one can win outright by surprise or threat. So, if someone tried it on and attacked, a counter-attack would not only still be possible, but would be so devastating as to make the aggressor impotent. In other words, the spoils of war would be spoiled, and war wouldn't be worth the pain or the prize. So no one starts it in the first place. This policy depends on the strategy known as MAD (Mutually Assured Destruction) which I touched on in an earlier chapter.

1. MAD—or NUTS?

Now, here's the first fundamental problem with the deterrent position. We have already moved away from MAD to what is equally appropriately termed NUTS (Nuclear Utilisation Target Selection). This has happened because of the growth and accuracy of nuclear weapons, also discussed in a previous chapter. Your second strike weapons, so necessary to deter a first strike from your enemy, are no longer invulnerable (anti-satellite and anti-submarine improvements have helped see to that), and consequently we now have strategies based on the possibility of winning a nuclear war through first-hit capabilities of great power and accuracy. This in turn has prompted the acceptance of a computer-determined 'launch on warning' strategy on both sides, because you can't afford the first (and now possibly only and therefore winning) 'shot' to be fired. The threshold of possible/probable war goes down all the time, not up. Once entertain the idea of your enemy or yourself winning a nuclear war, and deterrence is massively destabilised. NATO's 'flexible response' is based on this concept of waging any form of war on Europe, and has further blurred the distinction between a war being conventional, initially conventional, or nuclear. Nor will NATO declare a 'no first use' of nuclear weapons, reserving the right instead to use a nuclear bomb against conventional weapons in Europe before anyone else does. Once again the result of such a blurring is to reduce the effectiveness of deterrence. Deterrence only works if you know no one will use the bomb. What we are now saying is that someone might use the bomb first, and what's more, win by doing that.

2. *Time, Gentlemen, please!*

Deterrence also needs time if it is to work properly. There needs to be enough time for the awful consequences of pushing the world over the brink into nuclear holocaust to dawn on your government and military advisers. It was the tension of time that helped diffuse the Cuban missile crisis back in the 1960s. But today, with the speed of modern communications, of computerised decisions, of speeding missiles, planes, rockets, satellites, submarines and the like, we don't have time for measured, sober consideration. For one or both sides to back down, time is vital. And time is what we do not have.

Nor does deterrence deal realistically with what many political observers see as the worst period of tension between the USA and the USSR for thirty years. Many believe that we're back in the throes of the Cold War that began in the sixties. Although limitations on nuclear weapons and even disarmament agreements are being made, much tension is resurfacing between the superpowers. Certainly you won't hear talk of East-West detente anymore; that ended with the many expulsions of spies and diplomats from the USA, the UK and the USSR in the early to mid-eighties. We have Russian *glasnost* and *perestroika*, but these are more to do with internal changes and how acceptable they seem to the West than with relationships between the two.

The only recent concession to this overall situation has been a major one: the agreement (on and off and on as it has been) to ban intermediary, middle-range, middle-yield strategic weapons. This has also been followed by the promise of a considerable reduction in conventional forces in Europe by the USSR. These agreements are forged particularly in the provocative push forward in such areas as Cruise, Strategic Defence Initiative (Star Wars) and Trident in the United Kingdom rather than because of good relationships between East and West. We have much cause to be happy over what is currently happening in the armaments scene, but we have no cause to be complacent. Deterrence does not deal with any of these issues.

3. John the club

A further danger with deterrence is that it encourages the development and stockpiling of nuclear weapons.

Expansion doesn't just mean numbers of weapons, but the numbers of countries with nuclear weapons. As nuclear weapons are developed by minor powers, so the problems of deterrence increase: it's no longer a two-way stand off but a multiple one, fraught with the possibilities of imbalance. And with proliferation of the nuclear weapons and countries, the chances of nuclear bombs falling into the hands of some despotic maniac increases. Who'd want Libya's Colonel Gadhaffi or the IRA to wield such power?

4. 'There's many a slip...'

The more weapons, the more chance of error too. Deterrence, in allowing and promoting nuclear weapons, must take the blame for allowing and promoting the possibility of technical accidents, (like the explosion on the 18th May 1988 in a Ukraine SS24 nuclear missile fuel plant), and also the blame for possible human error. The arguments for deterrence point to the fact that it's the lesser of two evils (the other evil being war) because our world is fallen, yet at the same time deterrence makes no allowance in this imperfect and fallen world for the instability of human nature.

Not only does it make no allowance for accidental human error, but also tension-provoked psychological problems and deliberate human wickedness. For deterrence also provides opportunities for terrorists. Keep the bomb and you keep the possibility (ever increasing) of it falling into the hands of those who will use it, even if you won't. Even Ronald Reagan, former President of the USA, has admitted that the world can't go on for long without 'some fool or some maniac or some accident triggering the kind of war that is the end of the line for all of us' (*The Times*, 1983).

5. Peace in Europe?

As to whether deterrence works in providing peace, there are two issues here. The first is a common-sense one. You cannot prove that wars haven't happened because of nuclear weapons; it's impossible to prove that kind of negative. That's like saying, 'it didn't rain yesterday because I had my umbrella with me.' Or, 'it will rain today because I've left it at home.' It should also be impossible to argue from it logically! The nuclear bomb might have dissuaded war in Europe; or it might not. It might just as easily be increasing the tension, not deterring it. Indeed, there is every evidence that the Bomb hasn't prevented wars at all. The nuclear umbrella extends from the superpowers to their interests, and believing that nuclear war couldn't be risked has actually encouraged some wars rather than stopped them. As we've seen, the greatest danger here is that any war can escalate.

If deterrence is working to keep the peace, then what should we say to the Hungarians (1956), to the Czecho-slovakians (1948 and 1968), to the East Germans (1953), and to the Afghanistans (1979)? How about Angola and Cambodia? Or the Vietnam war, suc-cessfully fought by a non-nuclear force against a nuclear one? The USSR would want to ask the same questions about Cuba, the Middle East, South Amer-ica, Northern Ireland and the Falklands (more non-nuclear nations fighting nuclear ones).

To be free does not mean to be western, nor neces-sarily to live in a 'peaceful' nation. The best deterrence can produce is not freedom as peace but a balance of terror, and often it fails even to do that. Ten million have died in wars since the Second World War. There have been more than 250 wars since 1945, 17 of them still raging now. Have a look at God's warning on the

situation of false peace (Jer 8:15). There are frightening
parallels between the last forty or so years of so-called
peace since the Second World War and the forty years
of armed 'peace' between France and Germany before
the First World War. And that forty years of armed
peace (with the most ferocious weapons then available)
led to the most destructive war ever up to that point in
history. The cost was too great then in human life, but
it still happened. The comparison to today's armed
'peace' is obvious and disturbing.

We can't prove 'peace' has happened because of the
bomb. It hasn't happened anyway, even despite it. But
I said that there were two issues here. The second issue
lies in our very definition of peace. For the Christian,
peace isn't just a cessation of war. That would make
peace a negative thing, just a lack of aggression. In the
Bible peace has always been a much more positive force
than that. We saw earlier that in the Old Testament the
phrase which best summed up this concept of peace is
that Hebrew word *shalom*, used as a blessing: 'Peace to
you, peace be with you.' Ask any Jew what *shalom*
means and he'll tell you how much more it means than
'I hope you don't get in a fight today!' Old Testament
peace means 'live well, live in peace, be blessed, be
whole and happy and prosper'. It's a positive blessing
that encompasses the individual, his family and even
whole nations.

In the New Testament the idea of peace is the same,
but it's linked to the idea of being healed, made whole
or saved, so an approximate translation of the Old
Testament Hebrew *shalom* is the New Testament Greek
word *sozo*, meaning 'salvation'. It's a kind of positive,
forceful peace that is actually stronger than the storm of
conflict. When Jesus spoke creative words of faith (Mk
4:39), his command of peace stilled a storm! And his

disciples were given authority by Jesus to impart the same peace to households that received them (Lk 10:5).

In both Old and New Testaments, the source of peace is the same. Real peace clearly comes only from God—and when an individual and ultimately the world is in a right relationship with him. God is the author of peace, the God of peace. Real peace isn't lack of war or unused nuclear bombs or deterrence, it's the love of God in action when people lik you and me cease to argue against God's will for our lives. Jesus is the Prince of Peace. We can't desire that peace for others and not live it ourselves. Neither can we live it ourselves and then encourage others to violate God's will for peace for their lives. And that doesn't matter whether we're talking about individuals or nations.

6. Defence or destruction?

Deterrence isn't based on defence; it's based on destruction. The possible use of nuclear bombs is actually illegal, a fact little publicised by those who constantly decry the civil disobedience of people who demonstrate against the bomb. According to Article 48 of 'The Geneva Convention', 'warring parties shall at all times distinguish between the civilian population and combatants'. Now this is obviously impossible when it comes to nuclear war, making use, if not possession of the bomb, illegal.

7. Money well spent?

Before we go on to look at the specifically moral/Christian problems with using the bomb as deterrent, there's one final grave disadvantage with deterrence. It has squandered billions of pounds on arms that could've been far better spent on alleviating suffering, starvation and lack of education across the Third World. In the

UK we spend approximately £258 per head per year on NATO arms, deterrence and defence. That's the second highest amount (after the USA) of all NATO contributors. The government stated in one of its Ministry of Defence leaflets, dated March 1987, that 'it is NATO's aim to fulfil its deterrent role at minimum cost and with the fewest possible weapons'. Yet what of the £9000 Trident programme, which will increase fire power by a staggering and unnecessary fourteen times? This is indeed 'overkill'. Or what of our defence budget of £18.5 billion pounds being greater than our health budget at £17.7 billion?

What's more, deterrence has led to major nuclear powers like the USA, the USSR and the UK buying influence in developing countries through the escalation of the conventional arms trade. This has doubled over the last ten years with three quarters of all sales going to developing countries. According to the Bible, nations are judged not by their ability to defend themselves but by their trust in God, and by their treatment of the poor and the weak. Have a look at Matthew 25 verse 31 onwards. Basically deterrence diverts dosh! We further the gross inequality between the rich and the poor countries with our striving to provide a peace which isn't peace, by stockpiling weapons of mass destruction that are actually illegal to use and, as I hope we'll now see, from a Christian viewpoint, immoral to use.

Let's refute some of those Christian perspectives which I stated earlier that form the defence for the bomb as deterrent.

Countering the 'Christian' argument for deterrence

1. Fear and faith don't mix

First, the idea that the bomb, like the state, is both a product of and a remedy for the Fall. The idea is that God uses fear of nuclear bombs to deter nuclear war, taking our very folly and sinfulness and making the bomb an instrument of peace, of good. But where do we draw the line? Is God pro rape because it gives women a 'healthy' fear of walking the dog at night? Did God delight over the Inquisitioner's rack because it kept some from spreading heresy (it killed many true believers)? Of course God will work good out of bad alongside those who love and trust him, but that shouldn't be taken to mean that God gives a stamp of divine approval to evil. Or that evil somehow proceeds from God's very heart and will.

God is delighted we haven't had a nuclear war in Europe yet, but he hates the weapons of mass destruction and the fear they invoke. God is not a God of fear and terror: were you saved because of his love, or because of fear of hell? Of course, you could have been saved because of either, but I know which one God would rather. Will we settle for the minimum ('Oh well, God seems to be using fear of nuclear bombs, so we'll leave them be'), or do we aim for the maximum in God's heart ('What does He feel about bombs, war, hatred, violence, oppression, and what can we do?'). God's turning evil around to good purpose cannot be construed as God condoning evil—it's against his very nature.

2. Peacemakers, not peace-keepers

We cannot be uninvolved in the politics of it all because it's difficult, or divisive, or it will all happen anyway. Jesus never did that. He prophesied that the Temple in Jerusalem would be destroyed, but he still bothered enough to clear it out later! Our attitude to the earth's end should be to be good stewards of it now.

We are in a love relationship with God, his world, and each other which includes Christians and non-Christians. God's law on murder and rape isn't just for Christians. Nor is his law on love, forgiveness and peace just for Christians. Non-Christians may follow Christian ethics without the benefit of a renewed mind, and of the power of the Holy Spirit. But good things can still happen. Slavery has been abolished, children's work laws eased, hospices founded, education provided for many, and prisons reformed. All Christian initiatives carried out with the help of non-Christians.

Because we're in a love relationship with God, we will want to do what he wants us to do. And God wants us to establish his kingdom on earth in all its fullness— a kingdom where there is no pain, no sickness, no crying. We're called to be peace*makers*, not peace-*keepers*. Part of making peace involves resisting evil by legitimate means—bringing ourselves and others to conviction and repentance, and receiving the forgiveness and transforming love of God—and leaving the world's end, its how, why and when, to God (Mt 24:36–39).

3. National police force—international nukes?

We have a national police force internally, so why not have nuclear weapons internationally to deter wrong-doing and aggression? This sounds reasonable, but there's no real comparison. When we talk about peace-keeping within one nation, we are talking about individuals. A personal element is there. Of course, bombs which liquify millions, also liquify individuals. But on the whole, nuclear warfare takes on an inhuman tone and vast scale. The enemy becomes 'the reds'; strategies acquire neutral titles such as MAD and NUTS; cities of people, art, history and beauty become 'target centres'; warning systems sound reassuringly peaceful (DEW or Distant Early Warning systems), and so on.

Localised, internal, national disciplining through a police force is most rigidly enforced with a whole host of (not infallible) safeguards and checks. The police have certain powers we don't have as civilians, but we also have powers they don't, and they are subject to more rigorous checks than we are; they are not above the law, but embody the law. When we try to compare that with the international scene, especially in time of war or impending war, it won't work. There is no international, rational authority in times of crisis, so in war each nation becomes judge and law-enforcer—something that God never asked of anyone. The United Nations never stopped the USSR invading Afghanistan, nor could it. And it didn't stop our non-negotiation over the Falklands, nor could it. The biblical principle is that power and authority must be accounted for, and that applied even to the Son of God. Again and again Jesus makes the point that he recognises authority has to be accountable and that he himself is accountable to his Father and never does anything without his say so. Nationally, power and authority is accounted for. Internationally, power and authority isn't accounted for, nor can it be. One is not the same as the other. The only carry-over is the principle of love. That operates in individual, local, national and international spheres.

There is also a big difference between policing a riot, running a prison, rehabilitating offenders or protecting society, and wiping out a society, killing millions and ruining God's earth! Again, the two are not comparable. Leaving people alive at least provides them with options (surrender, reform, repentance, restitution, redemption). Killing them doesn't.

4. Can they or can't they?

It makes no practical or moral sense to me to argue that deterrence works because we all know that the weapons could never be used, yet it also works because we all know that they will be used in the event of war or threat of war. Neither does it make practical or moral sense to argue that deterrence can lead to growth in conventional arms that *can* be used. Conventional arms, which include gas and biochemical weapons of horrendous nature, are now devastatingly more destructive than those used in the First and Second World Wars, which killed 10 million and 55 million people respectively. How many people do we have to aim at killing before the deterrence factor takes over? Is it all right to kill fewer people with conventional weapons rather than nuclear ones? How many have to die before it's immoral?

5. Awkward questions

If we are going to accept the Bomb as deterrent then we as Christians have some difficult questions to answer. Are we saying that we are prepared to sacrifice everything—life, the earth, the future, the enemy—for what we believe is the best lifestyle, for freedom? 'Better dead than red'? Freedom and lifestyle isn't the only moral issue here, and at least survival provides opportunities for change, improvement, reconciliation and salvation, as pointed out earlier. Could it be that our values, our lifestyles and our nations have become idols? Could we be putting 'survival of our values' before the word of God? We'll look at what the word of God clearly says, as opposed to what tradition says, in the next chapter.

Are we willing, for the sake of such idols, to sacrifice whole nations as nuclear burnt-offerings? The reality is that there is good in every nation and that in the recreation of a new heaven and new earth, it will be the kings of the nations who will bring their glory (ie, those particular national emphases we all have, into the New Jerusalem [Rev 21:24]). Are we prepared to 'decimate' the body of Jesus Christ (the church), instead of following the clear teaching as laid down in Romans chapter 12 and 1 Corinthians chapters 12, 13 and 14 concerning our attitude to the church, local and worldwide? You might by some twist of logic and morality justify blowing up non-Christians even though they too are made in God's image, but could you ever justify blowing up Christians? Are we saying that we're willing (though not wanting) to destroy, for example, the church in the USSR, which has twice as many active Christians in it than there are in the United Kingdom? Do we trust God for our peace and our future, or do we trust nuclear bombs? Make no mistake, what you trust you come to worship: as Jesus said, 'Your heart will always be where your riches are' (Mt 6:21). By trust I don't mean a naïve 'trust God and it'll work out' mentality. That's irresponsible before God and each other, and is unrealistic about fallen human nature. But we can't be responsible before God while adopting positions which he's expressly forbidden and which are untenably immoral, such as I believe deterrence to be.

6. *Immoral use equals immoral threat*

This is the crux of the whole deterrence issue. Let's take it to the lowest common denominator on which most Christians would agree, be they just war or pacifist or deterrence orientated—and most are one of those three. If nuclear weapons are indiscriminate of military or civilian casualties, then it is immoral to use them. And if it's immoral to use them, then it's immoral to threaten to use them. John Stott's argument seems to bypass this as he maintains that the intention behind possession of nuclear bombs in deterrence is *not* to use them. But is this reasonable, or indeed realistic? I have no doubt that John Stott could keep a nuclear bomb in his back garden without the intention of using it—it would be theoretically merely a deterrent. But unfortunately all the governments' attitudes to deterrents militate against this.

You have to be willing to use nuclear weapons if you have them. Your intention must be to use them and you must be seen to have that capability and intention by your enemy, otherwise it's not deterrence: 'A country must possess the means to make it clear to any potential aggressor that it is capable of inflicting an unacceptable degree of damage in retaliation *and willing to do so*' (Ministry of Defence government leaflet, July 1985). And here is Stott's dilemma: non-intention to use equals non-deterrence; intention to use equals deterrence (of a limited sort, as we've already seen). But intention to do an immoral act equals an immoral act, as Jesus made very clear (Mt 5:28). John Stott's statement on intention is unfortunately at odds with our government's statement on (and any government's attitude to) deterrence. Deterrence is a trap: 'The nations have fallen into the pit they have dug; their feet are caught in the net they have hidden' (Ps 9:15).

To be really honest with you, I would have liked deterrence to have worked. I would have liked it to be morally defensible. In many ways deterrence seemed the best option, offering an uneasy balance of terror instead of peace. But as I hope we've seen in this chapter, not only is deterrence increasingly ineffective, it is also increasingly dangerous. The bomb cannot be good or used for good—it diverts money, faith and positive action. Not only that, it's immoral to use and therefore immoral to own and to threaten to use.

Deterrence in and of itself is *not* a bad thing, but we need to remember that only God can provide peace. However, nuclear deterrence in and of itself *is* a bad thing. Deterrence can only be a good thing when the thing that you threaten to do (where the threat acts as a deterrent) is not in itself immoral.

Nuclear bombing, mass genocide and the potential destruction of the world *is* immoral unless you are as just as God himself, and we're not.

The next two chapters will contradict and try to look beyond the 1987 United Kingdom Ministry of Defence leaflet which maintains that 'there is no alternative to nuclear deterrence as long as nuclear weapons exist'.

In the light of this overview of the biblical absolutes and practical models for peace, how can we fiddle about with situational ethics?

You see, situational ethics occur when we can't accept that God's absolutes are workable. You know what I mean. God says that he hates liars (Prov 19:22), but what do you do when faced with the hypothetical situation of an armed mad-man demanding to know which way the little girl ran whom he's pursuing to kill? After all, you've seen which way the little girl went. Do you lie? Tell the truth? Keep silent? Attack the mad-man? Often we choose to lie: the end justifies the means. But does it? If you lie, you become responsible for the outcome instead of God, who, after all, is much more capable of being responsible and working it out for good than you are. Any of the other three alternatives will do, for love for the mad-man can restrain and resist him, though never kill him. But they all cost more than lying does. Now God's absolutes work. But they cost.

God's absolutes always leave us with alternatives to doing wrong (have a look at 1 Corinthians 10:13).

All too often we do what God has already said we shouldn't do. The responsibility for the situation is then no longer God's but ours. When we delve into moral adjustments of God's absolutes, we display our lack of trust in His justice, mercy and power in complex situations. It's basically a question of who's the boss? Jesus when all is going swimmingly and us when we hit difficulties?

In the following chapter we will look at some of the positive alternatives to peacemaking that God provides us with.

8

The Way of Peace

It will probably have become obvious to you by now that I disagree radically with the positions on war and the bomb which we've looked at so far. However, it has not been easy for me to arrive at the position outlined in this chapter. I've had endless discussions, even arguments, over the theological basis for this stance. The arguments have mainly centred around the practicalities of a pacifist position, with questions like 'What would you have done in the Second World War?' 'Would you have let Hitler kill all the Jews?' Or 'Do you mean you wouldn't fight for your country in a war?' Sometimes the questions are more personal: 'But what if someone was about to rape and kill your wife?' Or 'Do you mean to say that if I punch you in the jaw right now you would just "turn the other cheek"?'

The option I seek to live by isn't an easy one. By the standards of the spirit of the age, it's a weak option. But I have to maintain that actually, for the Christian, it's not an option at all, it's the way.

In this chapter I'm going to suggest that pacifism is the way of Jesus Christ himself. His life, suffering, death and resurrection is our example as Christians, and because it worked for him it will work for us. The way of peace becomes the way of the cross. You cannot separate the two.

First, I'll look at God's character and his incarnation (Jesus Christ). Then I'll look at his means of working, and show how peace is a vital—not optional—part of all of that. Then I'll look at Jesus Christ's mission and his teaching on how to deal with your enemies, both personally, nationally and internationally. I'll also investigate teaching on peace and forgiveness in the New Testament other than Jesus' own direct teaching. I want to look at our whole approach to situational ethics, 'If this happens then what if....' I'd also like to look at what appear to be problem passages in the New Testament (we looked at the Old Testament problems in Chapter 5 under the heading of holy war) and see how these pose a stumbling block for the pacifist position.

The radical hero

We dare not forget how radical the teaching and lifestyle of our hero and model Jesus Christ really was all those two thousand years ago and four thousand miles away. Jesus broke into human history to make it history. He faced the political and powerful opinions of his day and rejected them all, instead ushering in a new way of living and dying. A kingdom-of-God way, that reverses world values (Lk 4:16–21), baffles the strong and apparently wise (1 Cor 1:20), and uses the weak and foolish for good (1 Cor 1:27).

It was no mere coincidence that Jesus came when he came, or to whom he came. The backdrop had been set for the Messiah to arrive. A people had been chosen, prepared and preserved miraculously by God all through the Old Testament, to provide a backdrop against which the brilliance of the coming Messiah, the Son of God, would clearly shine for all to see, although not for all to accept.

This Messiah entered human history at a time and a place of maximum communication possibilities. A through road, the growth of the Roman Empire, a widespread trade, governmental and language system existed. It was also a time and place of maximum persecution to a people oppressed for many years who expected a revolutionary, sword-wielding liberator, a warrior king Messiah.

Four options

The Jews had been oppressed for 300 years before Jesus came, first by the Greeks and then by the Romans. They were looking for a military Messiah. In fact, when the client King of Jerusalem, Herod the Great, died in 4 BC, three military 'messiahs' immediately arose to overthrow the Roman Government, with the result that 2,000 Jews were crucified. By the time Jesus got on the scene he had four political options open to him, as we saw in Chapter 3). He could go the way of the Sadducees and compromise with the authorities. Or he could go the way of the Pharisees who expounded the Law but made it a lie by the way they lived. Or he could hive off into the desert and start an alternative separatist community like the Essenes. Or he could take up arms and lead the Zealots as a freedom-fighter against the Romans. After all, the Zealots had affirmed in the Qumran community's 'manual of discipline' that 'whoever spills the blood of one of the godless is like one who offers a sacrifice'. For the Zealots it was perfectly in

order to 'love all the sons of light...and...hate all the
sons of darkness'.

Jesus was tempted to try these alternatives. The
temptation came not just from the world (Zealots or
Pharisee, Sadducees or Essenes), but also directly from
the enemy (Lk 4:1–13). For Jesus, there was only one
way to bring in God's kingdom and that was God's
way. Indeed, Jesus himself said that he was the way (Jn
14:6). And this truth is reflected in his teaching and
example.

A new way

This new way is the way of the Suffering Servant. It was
only new in that it had never before been 'fleshed out'
and fully demonstrated by a human being, or made
possible for others to follow. That was fulfilled in Jesus.
Actually this option of peace had always been there.
Violence had only come with the Fall, not before. It was
one of the first sins (have a look at Genesis 4:8 leading
on to Genesis 4:23–24 then go to Genesis 6:13). Before
Adam and Eve disobeyed God, even animals weren't
subjected to violence: mankind lived off plant life and
only after the Fall did God clothe people in animal skins
(Gen 3:21)—the first sacrifice for the sake of sin. And
right back then God had in mind his masterplan to
regain men and women through the work of his Son,
Jesus Christ. The prophet Isaiah clearly portrays the
suffering Servant King (Is 53). Other prophets tell the
same story: Jesus would be born to humility and to non-
violence (Zech 9:9). He would ride into Jerusalem on
an ass, not in a chariot (Lk 19:28–44). God's people
were to trust in God, not in weapons (Ps 33:16–19; Ps
18:8, 9). Warfare is a result of not going Jesus' way, so
it's clearly not an option for Christians, who are called

rather to salt society with peace. God warned that if his people (always primarily his people, and only then the rest of the world, [2 Pet 3:9]) continued in their sins then he would deliver them 'into the hand of their iniquities' (Is 64–67). It's a clear warning of what will happen if as Christians we try to create peace by a means which isn't God's way.

The gospel of peace

Jesus came to save, not to destroy (Lk 9:54–56). His whole mission was to proclaim the gospel (from the old English *godspell* meaning good news). The gospel is actually called the gospel of peace (Eph 6:15). Peace within the individual, peace among men. This peace— this shalom or wholeness—is an integral part of the gospel. It's the kingdom of God breaking in from the future to the present to redeem our past and change our destiny.

As you'd expect, no one was clearer about this mission of reconciliation, this bringing of peace, than Jesus Christ. He clearly knew that he was born to suffer (Mk 8:27–28), and He embraced all the horrors of that suffering willingly, though realistically and not gladly (Is 30:7, Mk 9:51, Lk 22:39–44). If there'd been another way, Jesus would have taken it. He knew that living and teaching forgiveness of sin, and peace with God, with yourself and with each other, wouldn't be received by all. That's the real meaning of the divisiveness of the Gospel in Matthew 10:34. Jesus knew the Jews, even his own disciples (Lk 9:51–56), wanted a military Messiah. Yet everything he did and said (Acts 1:1) showed this new way of dealing with your enemies at every level (personal, political, local, national and international). It was to be the way of costly, undeserved, unilateral (one way, unasked for) forgiveness. Have a look at Romans 5:8 and Luke 23:34. Right from the Old Testament onwards the blood came before the oil, sacrifice came before anointing, the Cross before Pentecost (see John 12:24–26). God's answer to violence and warfare is to be found, as you would expect, rooted in his character. It's the answer of selfless giving, of sacrificial love. It's unpleasant. It seems weak. It seems to fail in the short term. But it's the only long term solution. After the Cross, the Resurrection. After death, life. After laying down power, victory.

It's significant that Jesus' first public ethical teaching (to be found in Luke 6:27) consists of the command to 'love your enemy'. His teaching on peace, love and forgiveness is scattered throughout the four gospels and taken up as a major theme through the rest of the New Testament. It was, moreover, lived out by the early church for the first three hundred years of its existence, becoming one of the hallmarks that distinguished emerging Christian communities, and a source of conflict, complaint and grudging admiration from secular governmental authorities. You cannot ignore this clear and specific teaching. You can, however, reject it. You can try to argue that it only applies to the individual and not to governments. Or only to Christians and not to non-Christians. Or that 'times have changed'. But the words and lifestyle and cost paid by the Man of Peace echo across the centuries like an indictment of such rationalising and side-stepping. Let's look at some of these words then from one of the major passages on peace, love and undeserved forgiveness.

You have heard that it was said, 'eye for eye and tooth for tooth.' But I tell you, Do not resist an evil person. If someone strikes you on the right cheek, turn to him the other also. And if someone wants to sue you and take your tunic, let him have your cloak as well. If someone forces you to go one mile, go with him two miles. Give to the one who asks you, and do not turn away from the one who wants to borrow from you.

You have heard that it was said, 'love your neighbour and hate your enemy.' But I tell you: Love your enemies and pray for those who persecute you, that you may be sons of your Father in heaven. He causes his sun to rise on the evil and good, and sends rain on the righteous and the unrighteous. If you love those who love you, what reward will you get? Are not even the tax collectors doing that? And if you greet only your brothers, what are you doing more than others? Do not even pagans do that? Be perfect, therefore, as your heavenly Father is perfect (Mt 5:38–48).

Now these words are not one-offs. They are backed up by additional teaching (Jn 18:36, Mt 26:51, 52, Mt 22:17–22, Mt 5:9), and parallel passages in the other Gospels (for example, Lk 6:27–36). The teaching was to the crowds and to the disciples. The standard was for everyone, but especially for those who would call themselves disciples, or followers and learners, of Jesus Christ. In the Great Commission (Mt 28:20), Jesus told his disciples to teach to others everything he had commanded them to obey—and that included his words on peace.

Present or future?

But wait a minute. Wasn't Jesus' teaching an ethical system that was only for the future, when the kingdom comes in fullness? Not so. Jesus clearly saw himself as the Messiah (Lk 4:18–21). He stated many times that the kingdom of God was coming, was at hand, was within his disciples, and would be manifested in the lifetime of his believers (Lk 10:9; 17:21; Mk 9:1). His teaching on peace and forgiveness fulfils the Old Testament promises, prophecies and Law (Mt 5:17–26— look at the context!). It will be fleshed out and made possible in the present, but it will only be fully realised in the future.

We are living 'in between' times, between D-day and V-day. The decisive battle was fought and won by Jesus on the cross where he defeated Satan. That was D-day. V-day, Christ's triumphant return, still lies ahead. Meanwhile we are fighting not against flesh and blood, but a defeated yet still retaliatory foe—Satan and his demons. In all this we have to hold in tension the fact that Jesus' kingdom has come and is still coming.

Personal, national and international

Wasn't Jesus' teaching only for the individual? You can forgive someone who wrongs you, but not someone who wrongs another? You can forgive personal attacks but not national? You mustn't resist personal aggressors but you can resist national or international aggressors? But this is illogical. It's also impractical. And what's more it's unbiblical! We can see this when we look at what Jesus said, and at the context that he said it in. His words cannot be just for personal relationships. In Matthew 5:40 he specifically countermands the Mosaic Law quoted in the Old Testament, which was the judicial system. So his words here clearly apply to the State and to legal attitudes. Verse 41 is a specific reference to Roman military rule. The word 'force' used here means literally to requisition or seize by military and civil authorities, something the Zealots fought hard and violently against. The example given about going one mile refers to the practice of the Roman officers compelling Jews to follow the armies carrying equipment; a rule brought into force to compel Simon of Cyrene to carry Jesus' cross (Mt 27:32). So now the text has widened in context yet again. Now it's personal, legal/ state and military situations that demand peaceful, loving and forgiving reactions. This includes relationships between one ruling nation and one oppressed one. That's why it's no accident that Jesus came to a group of people who were so oppressed.

Jesus rescues us as individuals and as a people (Lk 1:71–75). His salvation is for sinful nations as well as individual sinful people. His commands thus apply to whole countries as well as individual men and women. This same Jesus denied that he was leading armed resistance (Lk 22:49–53). He backed up his claims with signs and wonders of peacemaking (Lk 22:51). He indicated that his methods and his goal, as shared by his disciples, were very different to the way of violence (Jn 18:36).

Unilateral forgiveness

The Cross is the supreme example of God unilaterally disarming himself (Phil 2:6, 7). It's the working out of the cost of Jesus' command to his disciples (that is, you and I) to love their enemies as God did (Rom 5:8–10). The Cross is much more than just a witness, to the folly of the sword, a kind of negative rebuke against violence, a 'look what a terrible mess violence will get you into'. It's the positive way to peace in our lives and in our nations. The Cross demonstrated for all time that God came not to revenge, but to forgive (Jn 3:16). At the cross of Jesus Christ truth and justice meet, in the face of opposition, cruelty, injustice in the Bible always met and countered by peace (see Psalms 94, 96, 97 and 100), threat, hatred and greed. We are commanded to have no less than the same attitude as Jesus Christ (Phil 2:5). Dare we be pacifist? In the light of the Father's heart, of Jesus' example, of the teaching of the Bible, and of the power of the Holy Spirit, dare we be less?

The resurrection of Jesus meant that his way of peace was possible and would eventually triumph. Peace marked his resurrection gift to his disciples in that fear-ridden, oppressed upper room (Jn 20:19–21). Often we end up being scared of being weak, yet power, and trust in power threatens safety rather than ensures it—check out Luke 11:21, 22. Only Jesus' power to love is safe. Only the defenceless can make peace; they are not a threat, nor are they arrogant. They rely not on self but on God. How can 2 Corinthians 12:9–10 square up with the keeping of nuclear arsenals?! The New Testament is full of references to the living out by later Christians of the 'Jesus example'. Justice, peace and joy are, according to Romans 14:18, hallmarks of God's very kingdom.

Our calling

As Christians we're called to seek and pursue peace (1 Pet 3:8–12), just as Jesus did (see the superb description in 1 Pet 2:19–25). We have been given a ministry of reconciliation (2 Cor 5:18–19). We are bringers of the gospel of peace. God's grace, released to us in the New Covenant through Jesus, means that now evil is reserved for God's judgment, and not for us to punish. It is our responsibility to bless our enemies (Rom 12:14–21), rather than make them, and to cultivate peace—the fruit of the Holy Spirit—in our lives.

Difficult passages

But what about the seemingly difficult passages in the Gospels and the New Testament letters which seem to indicate that Jesus did not embrace total pacifism?

1. The cleansing of the temple (Jn 2:13–16, Mt 21:12–13 and Mk 11:15–17)

Surely Jesus employs violence here (a whip) to punish people? We need to look more closely at the text yet without manipulating it. For a start, this can't have been a physical attack on people by Jesus or he would've been arrested. Secondly, the phrase used for Jesus 'driving out' the people is rather a harsh translation—in Matthew 9:38 the same phrase is translated as 'sends out' workers. Thirdly, John 2:15 makes it clear that the whip was used on animals, not people. It was Jesus' tongue that lashed the sellers. Finally, Mark 11:17 indicates that Jesus was in part objecting to nationalism. The area of the temple which Jesus was clearing was specifically for non-Jews, who were being abused by the Jewish money-changers and sellers of animals for sacrifice. This incident therefore becomes a poor argument for backing the use of nuclear threat to protect our own nation, when all too often nationalism can be our motive.

2. 'Wars and rumours of wars' (Mt 24:6)

If Jesus said that wars would happen, how can nuclear weapons be out of his will? Well, much happens that is out of his will. People die unsaved (see 2 Pet 3:9), but this doesn't mean that (a) it's good because it happens or (b) we shouldn't bother to try and affect it because it happens. We continue to resist persecution of the Christian Church, we don't plead to be martyred, we don't encourage brothers to hate brothers, or children their parents—all things which are mentioned by Jesus in the very same passage. If we resist those things then why not resist war? We also need to realise that Matthew 24:6 doesn't actually say that war and rumours of war will continue up until Jesus comes, though they probably will; it's certainly not a verse to encourage fatalism and apathy.

3. 'If you don't have a sword...buy one' (Lk 22:35–38)

Jesus clearly tells his disciples to buy a sword. Surely this passage has to be in support of violence or at the least, violent self-defence and resistance? The real problem is that if it does mean that, it's not logical. For in the same passage Jesus quotes some of the words about the Suffering Servant (Is 53:12), hardly in keeping with a directive to fight! If Jesus were advocating armed rebellion, two swords would certainly not be 'enough'. You also have to balance this passage with the general tenor of Jesus' attitude: his rebuke to Peter's violence at Gethsemane only a little later (Lk 22:51), and his telling Pilate that his disciples don't fight (Jn 18:36). So if Jesus couldn't have meant 'arm yourself to fight', what did he mean? All that is clear is what he couldn't have meant without contradicting himself elsewhere. Probably the talk of swords is to provide a vivid picture of the fact that there was to be trouble ahead, much as we might say 'You're going to get into hot water' without expecting people to jump into kettles! It has been strongly suggested that Jesus said 'It is enough' that he meant (that is, his tone implied) 'Enough of silly talk about using real swords. Don't you understand? Don't be so stupid!'

4. Soldiers

If war and violence are so wrong why aren't soldiers, who are mentioned several times in the New Testament (for example, Matthew 8:10 and Acts 10) condemned? To follow in the vein of this argument prostitution and theft are mentioned in Luke 7:36–50 and 23:39–43 but neither are condemned! But does this mean that they are therefore permissible. Both are condemned specifically elsewhere in Scripture. And both go against God's character revealed in the general drift of the Bible too. It is the same with violence and war—as backed up by 300 years of practice by the early church, as well as the clear teachings of Jesus and the apostles.

5. 'I did not come to bring peace, but a sword' (Mt 10:34)

This passage needs to be read in context (verse 25–42) where Jesus is talking of spiritual division based on moral choice (ie, for or against him), not physical division based on violence.

6. 'Do not resist an evil person' (Mt 5:39)

Didn't Jesus resist evil people. What about the Pharisees in Matthew 23:13–29, or the temple moneychangers in Mark 11, or the guard who slapped him during his trial in John 18:19–24. Jesus certainly resisted evil (as indeed we are commanded to in James 4:7), but his resistance clearly doesn't mean exacting equal revenge, or making your opponent an enemy, even though at great personal cost. The purpose of this resistance is reconciliation (have a look at Galatians 6:1–2 and 1 Corinthians 5:5) where the best interests of your opponent come first (which can't mean nuking him!). Jesus' resistance is marked more by what he doesn't do than by what he does.

7. Military images

Sometimes in the New Testament, for example Ephesians 6:10–17 and 2 Timothy 2:3, we find word pictures drawn from military life. This wouldn't happen, it's sometimes argued, if military might was wrong! What, then, can we say about other passages, such as Ephesians 5:18 where being filled with the Holy Spirit is equated to being drunk; Matthew 24:43 where Jesus is pictured as a thief, or Luke 18:1–8 where God is depicted as an unjust judge? Bear in mind that these military pictures relate to heavenly conflict, not to 'flesh and blood' (Eph 6:12).

8. Submission to government

Romans 13, with its parallel passage in 1 Peter 2:13–14, is perhaps the thorniest of the so-called problem passages. We need to look closely at this passage because it's the one most quoted by fellow Christians to support obedience to the State war-machine, and it seems to demand just that. To place the passage in full context we need to read from Romans 12:9–13:14.

If we read Romans 13 simply and directly as a command to obey any and every government then we have immediately got problems on a number of biblical and moral fronts. 'Be subject to government' can't just mean 'Christian, be subject to a Western government, but don't be subject to Russian government'! If it's a straight command then it's a straight command for all. However, that can't be right, for it would mean that God through Paul is potentially commanding Christians in the West in the event of war to hate and kill Christians in the East at their respective government's orders. Yet everywhere else in Scripture we're commanded to pray for, give to and love the saints to be a true 'body'. Moreover, we're also commanded to love our enemies, never mind just our fellow Christians! 'Be subject to government' can't be right for one nation and wrong for another! So what does it mean?

I suggest that the point Paul is trying to make, especially as it's placed in the context of love and forgiveness and not taking revenge, is that Christians should exercise non-retaliatory love towards the governments over them, and towards other people, even when it hurts. Have a look at Romans 12, 14, 17, 19 and 20 and Romans 13:8–10. Remember that Paul is writing to Christians in Rome, the heart of an oppressively anti-Christian empire. His point is, that being subject to government means you can't just destroy government or obey government to destroy one another! Paul is commanding restraint not retaliation. His is an argument for peace, not retaliation. In addition, this passage doesn't refer to warfare in its commands, but internal policing. The two are different, as we saw earlier. Only Jesus' law of love and forgiveness can cover the personal, local, national and international. The law of love and forgiveness is universal.

There are times when the Bible makes a command which seems to accept the status quo. This in turn seems to give room for an evil abuse of that command to flourish (for example, slaves submit to your masters in 1 Peter 2, children to parents, and wives to husbands in Ephesians 5, people to governments in Romans 13). However, every time the Bible makes such a command, it does so in the context of redeeming love (1 Pet 2:19–24; Eph 5:21, 25–33; 6:4; Rom 12:14–21; 13:8–14). Love is the goal of power, discipline, subjection and submission, coercion *and* resistance. It is both the end *and* the means. It is for family, church, state, relationships, employment, the military, judiciary and international affairs. So the goal of resistance is not to destroy governments but to improve them. That is Paul's real point in Romans 13, clearly seen when placed in the context of Romans 12.

But is Paul actually saying we can resist? Look more closely at the text. The command is to be 'subject' to government, not to 'obey' government (only the Good News Bible and the Living Bible have the word 'obey', and they shouldn't have!). The New Testament Greek word is *hupotassein* which means 'submit' or be 'subject to'; not the Greek word *hupakonein* which means 'obey'. We're not playing with words here. In the New Testament the word in Romans 13:1 occurs thirty times, and for the vast majority of times it is not translated 'obey'. Its equivalent (Hebrew) word in the Old Testament occurs twenty-one times, but only once is it translated 'obey'. So you can be subject or submitted to government and yet not obey it. When?

The answer is as you would expect: when the government tells you to do something which is against God's will, or forbids you to do something which is God's will—such as worship or evangelism. Then you can disobey the government (this is civil disobedience) and yet remain subject to it. You are not trying to wrest power violently from a government or destroy that government, but rather you are trying to obey God and improve government. For God works through governments and only he destroys and elects them. So if you obey God and disobey the government, you pay the price (a fine, imprisonment, in some places torture and death) because you're still subject to it. Submission and subjection to government means you accept the consequences of disobedience where disobedience is necessary. It certainly does not mean blind disobedience. There are lots of precedents in the Bible for disobeying government. Jesus was subject to the state (Mt 17:24–

27), and yet he resisted it (Mt 21:12). He never attacked
Caesar or formed a political party, but his actions were
political because they made room in mens' lives for the
rule of the King, and for this he was charged with
sedition.

Being subject to government means we can and
should demand just action in our judiciary (Acts 16:37–
39; 24:10; 25:10–11). Yet it also means we obey God
before men (Acts 4:19–20; 5:29; Mt 22:17–22). This
happened in the Old Testament as well as the New.
Daniel and his friends disobeyed King Nebuchadnezzar
(Dan 3 and 6); the Hebrew midwives disobeyed Phar-
aoh and saved Moses (Ex 1:16–21); Joseph disobeyed
Potiphar's wife (Gen 39:6–10); the Jews disobeyed the
government of Persia (Esther 3:2–7); and Esther her-
self disobeyed (Esther 4:10–16). This has happened in
our own recent history many times. Corrie Ten Boom
saved the lives of scores of Jews and allied soldiers in
occupied, war-torn Holland. And it will happen again,
according to Revelation chapter 13.

If we don't take this line, which is in agreement with
Romans 13, the rest of Scripture and the character of
God, then we are in danger of developing too high a
view of government. We accredit governments with the
same power as God to judge rightly and righteously
(which are two different things—it's possible to be
right but have the wrong attitude and therefore not be
righteous). We might even do far worse and accredit
governments with the power to exercise vengeance and
to kill. We then back our own actions by saying we are
carrying out God's actions against evil and the devil.
This is a distortion that none of us can afford.

Governments exist to benefit you and do you good as
you in turn do good. Do evil and a good government
will punish you, as will your conscience. But let a

government punish you for doing good and for obeying
God and the scene switches. You may then disobey it,
though you should still be subject to the consequences
of your disobedience. And God will deal heavily with
those in authority who misuse their power to do ill
rather than good.

In 1988 the United Kingdom's government finally
enforced its previous decision that working for national
security at General Communications Headquarters
(GCHQ) was incompatible with trade union membership. The reason? Because it would cause a conflict of
political loyalties. Whether you think that's right or
wrong, if the government can see such a conflict of
interests, why can't the Christian? We must be
ruthlessly honest with ourselves. Which kingdom comes
first—the United Kingdom or God's? What are we
defending and at what cost? Can't it be said that
because of a conflict of loyalties there are some things
(global annihilation, nuclear arsenals, nuclear warfare,
violence, killing and maiming, threat and hatred) that a
Christian cannot be party to?

In the light of this overview of the biblical absolutes
and practical models for peace, how can we fiddle about
with situational ethics? Situational ethics only occur
when we cannot accept that God's absolutes are workable. But God's absolutes are in fact workable,
although they're costly. They always leave us with
alternatives to doing wrong (see 1 Corinthians 10:13).
All too often we do what God has already said we
shouldn't do. The responsibility for the situation is then
no longer God's but ours. When we delve into moral
adjustments of God's absolutes, we display our lack of
trust in his justice, mercy, and power in complex situations. It's basically a question of who's boss. Jesus

when all is going swimmingly, and us when we hit difficulties?

In our final chapter we will look at some of the positive alternatives for peacemaking that God provides us with.

9

Eating the Elephant

Practical Alternatives to Nuclear and Military Defence

Christian pacifism, far from being negative, must affect us at every level of our lives: from the personal to the international. Christian pacifism must affect us on the personal level because it's the individual's obedient response to the commands of his Boss, Jesus Christ. It must also affect the church because it's the result of a right response to each other as Christians in community—and to our enemies. It affects our evangelism because it's part of the good news of Jesus Christ. Christian pacifism springs from the Holy Spirit because without his renewing and empowering, it cannot be realised. Christian pacifism is a vital part of the kingdom of God, for it brings peace here and now to Christians in the church, and beyond the church to the world. And when the kingdom finally comes in fullness, peace will come in fullness too.

Ambulance or Fence

If you've reached this chapter, after all the arguments of the previous eight, and now find that you agree with me that Jesus' way is the only way to find peace, then by now, like me, you should be crying out for alternatives. As Christians we shouldn't be content to wait at the bottom of the cliff of world affairs, waiting for the world to hurl itself lemming-like off the top while we smile smugly and say, 'I told you so,' and pick up the pieces. There is certainly a need for the church to come to the rescue of the nations, rather like an ambulance, and heal and restore them.

But there's an even more fundamental role for the committed Christian and his church. We need to be a fence at the top of the cliff, not just an ambulance at the bottom! We will not just offer a social service like feeding the poor and freeing the oppressed, but radical social action—asking questions and setting agendas: why are people poor; why are they oppressed? The aim of such action is not Utopia, but a realistic improvement of the current situation while waiting for the return of Jesus Christ. In this chapter I want to look at what will make strong foundations for that fence— strong enough to stop the world going over the brink.

Growing pains

There are five main parts which make up the framework for this fence. They will stop us from washing our hands of Jesus and his command to love God and our neighbour as ourselves, even when our neighbour is our national enemy! John Stott lists these five areas very helpfully in his book *Issues Facing Christians Today*.

God

The first area that needs expanding is the size of our God. Do we believe in a God who is totally involved with all people, full of loving care towards them? God's

heart is not only with the 11% who are to be found fairly
regularly in churches throughout the United Kingdom,
but also with the 89% who aren't! That's a lot of heart!
The story of God's involvement with his world starts in
the Bible with Adam, not with Abraham who was
chosen. It starts with the nations, not with the chosen
people Israel. It starts with creation, not with covenant
and recreation. (Have a look at Amos 9:7, Daniel 4:32
and Psalm 33:13–15.) God has always demanded justice from all nations, not just from Israel (see Amos 1:2,
or Nahum's story.) Consequently all sense of injustice
comes from God (Rom 2:14, 15). We need a bigger
God—to see him more as he really is.

People

Secondly, we need a bigger view of people, to understand that they are all created in God's image and they
all have dignity due to them. For too long we have
thought, and therefore acted, as though human beings
were totally corrupted at the Fall: the truth is that every
part of the human being was corrupted, but the human
being wasn't totally corrupted. Vestiges of the image of
God can be found in Christians and non-Christians
alike, and all have dignity—or should have. God wants
to redeem our humanity, not deny it. You and I therefore owe no less to one another, regardless of nationalism (look at Genesis 9:6 and James 3:9).

Jesus

Thirdly, our view of Jesus Christ must expand. We
must look again at the Incarnation, the most powerful
expression of God's total and passionate involvement
with humanity. This close involvement has always been
God's way of working in both Old and New Testaments. The church, filled with the Holy Spirit, is now

the body of Jesus Christ on earth. We are sent just as he was sent, as an involved suffering servant.

Salvation

Fourthly, salvation is a more incredible reality than we often realise. It's not just for the individual, but also for the community (the church), and through that community for society. In this way, God's kingdom will be brought in. Jesus is referred to as Lord in the New Testament approximately nine times more than he is referred to as Saviour. Where Jesus reigns, he saves (Is 52:7; Mk 10:24–26). The atheist philosopher, Nietzsche, said, 'His disciples will have to look more saved if I am to believe in the Saviour.' It is the church's responsibility, as a body of saved people, to declare that salvation to the governments of the world, to declare that Jesus Christ is King. Jesus' salvation seen in us puts flesh and blood on that message.

The church

Finally, we need a bigger mind and heart for the church. If we know that it's not a building why do we keep on behaving as though it is? Why do we exhaust our energies and maintain a false loyalty if we're propping up something that isn't really church at all, and should've been allowed to fall over (many so-called 'churches' are dead on their feet anyway!) long ago? Why have we made it all so religious when Jesus hated religion? The Greek word for church is *ecclesia*, which means a like-minded body of people. This non-religious word, used of the crowd who stoned Stephen to death (Acts 7), is really a verb not a noun! We 'church it' together when together as the people of God we think right, live right, adapt to meet needs, love God and one another, share 'friendship' together and so on (Acts

2:42–47). It's time you and I got the world out of the church and got the church into the world (Mt 5:13–16, 1 Pet 2:11–17)!

Before we go on to look at practical alternatives to war and violence can we nail dead that lingering feeling that 'it's all right for us as Christians to believe there's an alternative, but we have to live in a tough, largely non-Christian world. And anyway, should we even impose our views on those who don't share our world-view and value system?'

The church is called to be holy, which means set apart. We have the example of Jesus to follow, the power of his Spirit to help us, and positive alternatives to the world's methods in the waging of our aggressive warfare (see Mt 5:38–48; Rom 12:17–21; 13:8; Jas 4:7; 1 Pet 2:21–24; 5:9).

As we try to live out these alternatives we need to steer a route between the two wrongs of 'imposition' (making the wretched pagans believe that we are right, and if they don't, making them live our way anyway!) and apathy. Neither of these two extremes have ever worked. Imposition through the Church bred the Inquisition between the thirteenth century and 1874— and who wants that back? Imposition through politics leads to absolutism, to despots and tyrants, or even in a democracy to something like the shambles of Prohibition in the USA (1920–1933), when alcohol was banned in an unenforcable law that bred gangsters like Al Capone.

Apathy in the Church gave Hitler and the Third Reich a virtually unopposed hate campaign against the Jews. Apathy in politics leads to anarchy and a minority ruling the lazy majority to no good ends. Imposition, and apathy are both wrong.

The persuaders

Our course must occupy the middle ground of persuasion. This acknowledges God's costly gift of free will to us, and therefore leaves everyone involved the possibility of choice. The totally reasonable, totally right God takes this route with the totally unreasonable, totally wrong world (Is 1:18). Through persuasion the church can become the conscience of the nation to educate that nation. Politicians instinctively know this when they demand moral leads from the church, as in recent months. They also get instinctively threatened when the church makes moral statements on political issues, like trade unionism, poverty and defence. But that's no bad thing. Because the Law of God is in the heart of man and people know what is sinful (Rom 2:14 onwards), conscience can lead us to make a right choice, and people groups can be persuaded that a right choice is in their self-interest—that it's good as well as godly to adopt just and peaceful laws. In all this there is a tension between idealism and realism.

So we can and should be involved, though our attitudes are vital. Now, how practically can we be involved? There are daring initiatives to be taken at every level. Have we got the guts?

Actions and reactions

Of course, at the end of the day the United Kingdom can only be held responsible, as can each individual, for its own actions and reactions. The United Kingdom isn't and can't be responsible for the actions and reactions of another nation, such as the USSR. We can and should be aware that our actions and reactions might provoke another country to either righteousness or unrighteousness. But beyond that, our responsibility is to look to our own actions and reactions. Even to be provoked does not remove the onus of responsibility for reactions from us.

Many of the stalemates in the arms race are a result of people trying to be responsible for other peoples' reactions and not being daring enough to be responsible for their own actions. We need to make bold and generous gestures of peace; as Pope John Paul II said in 1979, 'Make gestures of peace, even audacious ones. Break free from vicious circles.' We also need to find viable alternatives to the arms race, and to deny the Ministry of Defence 1987 leaflet which maintained that 'There is no alternative to nuclear deterrence as long as nuclear weapons exist.' With simple and unerring accuracy, Jim Wallis in *The Call to Conversion* sounds the warning for Christians: 'Doctrines of demons now have us believing that it's lunacy to put down your weapons.' The issue isn't between violence or non-violence, but between non-violence or non-existence! It's not between action or non-action, but between action and right action. We are not to be non-combatants who abandon the world to its own (nuclear) devices, derive benefit from the unholy mess, and service war by our very inaction. Instead we must seek out right action.

What is right action for the Christian?

Begin at the beginning

To be realistic, we must aim to take governments from where they are to where they conceive they could be, and then on to where they never thought possible— that is, as near to the kingdom of God as possible. Negotiating from superior strength is unlikely to encourage governments to shift in anything but the wrong direction, whereas negotiating from unilateral towards multilateral disarmament is, I believe, more viable. Unilateral initiatives should be more likely to come from Western governments because we claim that our arsenals are only defensive, that we have no goal of world domination, and that democracy is a better system than communism. Which is more risky: unilateralism or the present proliferation of nuclear weapons? It's worth bearing in mind that no unilateralist is against multilateralism. But why stop there? Let's go for broke!

Abandoning 'righteous rhetoric', which is simplistically pro 'us' and anti 'the enemy', and less talk of 'evil empires' will be a move towards the kingdom of God. The talks on arms reductions were one result of ex-President Reagan's dropping his previous righteous rhetoric. And arms reductions are a step nearer God's ideals than arms freezes. An arms freeze would be a start (so that the USSR doesn't build its planned new heavy bomber, and the manufacturing of three nuclear bombs per day in the USA ceases). And making the East/West border nuclear free would certainly be a move in the right direction. We've already moved from the realms of the desirable into the actual with the first ever arms reductions in 1989. Why not go further? Isn't a nuclear-free East/West border at least conceivable? Imagine a nuclear-free Europe. How about renouncing independent nuclear weapons (for example, the United Kingdom's) and removing USA bases from the United Kingdom? This isn't merely to suggest that the UK becomes neutral, only concerned selfishly with its own national protection. Rather, by making initial moves, Great Britain might become truly great in the kingdom of God by serving others and setting a lead, albeit a risky one. We could make a positive step out of joining the 'membership club' of the 152 nations without the bomb. These are choices for life and blessing (Deut 30:19), not for death and cursing.

A bite at a time

There are three levels at which we need to apply principles to practice. The personal level, the church level, and the national/international level. The latter, which seems so huge as to be beyond us, will never happen unless we start first with the personal. It's the old question 'how do you eat an elephant?' Answer 'a bite at a time.' We can't change everyone's life everywhere, but we can change someone's life somewhere, and we might as well start now. So first, the personal level.

The power of non-violence is a viable alternative. To be a pacifist doesn't mean negatively to be passive, but positively to be a peace-maker (Eph 2:14–16). The power of non-violence lies in five propositions summed up by Christian pacifist Martin Luther King and paraphrased here by me.

1. Non-violent resistance isn't for wimps; it's not the easy route.
2. It doesn't aim to defeat or humiliate the opponent, but rather aims to win understanding, mutual respect and friendship.
3. It attacks actively, positively and aggressively—forces, not people.
4. It accepts suffering without retaliation (that's one reason why it's not for wimps or bullies!).
5. It avoids external physical force and rejects internal violence of spirit.

If only we in the church would fight as hard for the gospel of peace and as hard against leading comfortable lives as we all too often fight for nationalism and war-like stand offs. To rely on nuclear weapons is to despair that change can ever happen, and to use them denies that change for all time. This is a kind of practical atheism. We dare not deny the problem, we dare not degenerate the problem (through oversimplification) and we need not despair of the problem. Instead, to rely on God, our personal alternative must start with prayer.

Prayer

Hang on a minute! Surely prayer is just a cop out? We're talking the real, hard, aggressive world here. Big money. Power. Leadership. Governments and nationalism at stake. In such a context prayer can seem like escapism. But I think that says more about my prayer life than about the very real and dynamic power of prayer. God wants to teach us how to pray so that he can answer our prayers with a 'yes'. He doesn't want to have to say 'no'; he wants us to ask for the right things for the right reasons in the right way (see Lk 11:13, Jas 4:1–3, Jn 15:16). Then he *can* say 'yes'. If my prayer life isn't working, it's the pray-er that's got it wrong, not God or the means of prayer itself. Prayer will actually involve the pray-er more, not less. In Matthew 9 Jesus Christ told his disciples to pray for workers for the harvest. He then went on to spring the news (in Matthew 10) that God had heard and answered their prayers and the answer to the prayer in this case was the pray-ers. The disciples became the workers and were sent out into the harvest.

Prayer isn't impractical because (a) God answers prayers, (b) God teaches us to pray, (c) God changes people who pray, and (d) God uses those who pray. We are specifically commanded to pray for those in authority over us (1 Tim 2:2)—and for our enemies (Mt 5:44). The apostle James wrote that 'the prayer of a righteous man is powerful and effective' (Jas 5:16). Prayer is the first step in Christian warfare. We need to identify where the battle is, and pray in a way that will affect the earthly situation (see Eph 6:10–18). Prayer is certainly not inaction, for spiritual warfare is about binding and loosing in the heavenlies in order that it might be accomplished tangibly on the earth. Start praying and then ask for something that will require more faith than you have. God will change the prayer fuse capacity in you so that you can take a bigger charge of his power, so you will go from being a 3 amp pray-er to a 5 amp to a 13 amp pray-er! This is a part of what Kenneth Greet, in his suggestions on alternatives to warfare for the Christian, calls 'inspiration'—it deals with our personal involvement in the peace-making process.

So here's a practical first alternative: pray. Get on the mailing list of your local Christian CND movement. Do your own Bible study on peace (use a concordance, a commentary and a notebook, and perhaps this book too). Start a Pray for Peace prayer diary, pasting in newspaper clippings on arsenals, wars and 'near incidents', and praying over them. Pray for your government, your Defence Minister, and your local MP. Get prayers for peace introduced into your church prayer meeting every week and go there yourself. Start a weekly prayer triplet to pray for world peace. Or target before God one war-torn country (Angola, Cambodia, Afghanistan, Northern Ireland, Beirut and the Middle East, etc) and pray for it.

Where is the light? Where is the salt?

Secondly, you'll soon notice that peculiar quality of real prayer: it starts to challenge your attitudes. This is vital if you and I are to become peacemakers, like Jesus. As Christians we are called to be light and salt in the world. But we will not be effective if things are wrong within us. To be a peacemaker you must be at peace with yourself. Peaceful alternatives start with personal conversion, to Jesus Christ, and to his attitudes, life-style and teaching. For this reason evangelism is a practical part of peace-making. If more radical evangelism was done we'd probably see more evangelism banned, because it would be seen as promoting peace and being 'anti-defence' or even 'anti-patriotic'. Personal repentance and conversion will change us. Our minds will be transformed, leading to a radical lifestyle (Rom 12:1–3). We will begin to have the same attitude as Jesus Christ (Phil 2:5). Although we will be reasoning very firmly in the present reality, we will seek to learn from the mistakes of the past, and our perspective will be an eternal one. We will be aware of evil, and clued in to some of Satan's strategies. We will remain true to Jesus Christ's revelation and accept the authority of the Creator God and his word, yet not allow 'principle' to over-ride our compassionate concern for individuals. God has given you and me a mind to use, a text-book (the Bible) to read, a teacher (the Holy Spirit) to guide us and a school (the church) to learn in. We need to draw on them all to find viable alternatives to war! We must be salt that hasn't lost its saltiness; light that does shine. People at peace.

Dealing with roots

All this will mean that after prayer, we will allow the Holy Spirit to root out of us those things that make for war against peace: things like insecurity, strife within families and within our other relationships, our over-affluent lifestyles at the expense of others, and—yes—nationalism.

We will need to take a fresh look at our understanding of pacifism, asking the Holy Spirit to root out pre-conceived ideas. These ideas could be that pacifism is too liberal an interpretation of the gospel. A kind of 'brotherhood of man' without the transforming power of personal repentance through Jesus Christ. Or that pacifism smacks of a very wish-washy social gospel—salvation and peace by works. Or that pacifism is a waste of time and energy because only Jesus Christ's return will do any good.

What about our attitude to our society. Are we firmly pro the status quo to defend a comfortable middle-class lifestyle, and the Third world can go to the wall? Or are we cynical, disillusioned with humanity and the potential it has created for huge scale destruction? It is these things that make for war within us. Peace doesn't lie in bombs, in NATO or in treaties. Peace lies in our hearts by the grace of God. Our tools are forged in the fire of God's love—the love of a father for his children bringing security; the love we enjoy through friendship with Jesus Christ and the forgiveness that brings, and the love of the Holy Spirit who changes us within. They are tools of love, prayer, truth, justice, wisdom, courage, forgiveness, security and self-sacrifice.

The only conflict that births this kind of peace is the conflict of the cross of Jesus Christ. This has always been God's kind of conflict; the giant Goliath against the boy David. The seemingly insignificant mustard seed. Using the humble, the weak, the foolish, the poor. Making ploughshares from swords. Overthrowing evil in men's lives by the birth of a helpless baby one night in Jerusalem. (Look at Isa 53:7; Mt 5:9, 38–48; Lk 6:27–36.)

It's prayer that reveals to us our inner thughts and attitudes, prayerful revelation will wake us up out of our indifference, lulled as we can be by such sanitised terms as nuclear 'clean bombs'. Or the missile called 'Bambi'. Or the cosy 'nuclear club'. Or the comforting 'nuclear umbrella'. Prayer will show us what God thinks of an MX missile called by ex-President Reagan the 'peace missile' and 'peacekeeper'! Or of the United States strategic air command motto 'Peace is our profession.' And even what God's heart is towards a Christian organisation which is pro-cruise missiles in the United Kingdom and which can call itself 'Shalom'!

'Oh God, root out our indifference as we pray. Change our hearts. Save us from being anaesthetised by incomprehension, by fear and hopelessness, or by embarrassment to speak out. Save us from dwelling too much on the macabre nature of possible nuclear disaster. Holy Spirit of God, make our hearts sensitive again.'

Politics

Personal involvement means that we can also participate in the political process. One day, you may be called to participate directly in this process. Take encouragement from people such as William Wilberforce who helped to abolish the slave trade. Other Christians have waged war through political persuasion and prayer, helping to overthrow child abuse and homelessness, and inhuman working hours for children (Barnado, Booth, Mueller). We have prison reform (Fry), the provision of schooling, hospitals and hospices (Nightingale). The fight against leprosy, against the exploitation of coffee plantation workers in Ghana, against castes in India, and against crippling foot-binding in China. Of course, we may not ever be called to such work in parliament, but we can lobby our MPs with letters of commendation and disapproval (both please). Find out who your MP is. Visit his local 'clinic', and ask him about his views on defence, nuclear war and weapons, Trident, NATO etc. Be gracious, but be clear. Make only one point per letter or visit. Don't be aggressive, even in disagreement. But do participate.

Media

How about crashing the local media? There's often access to local radio, local newspapers and 'freebies'. Type a neat, short (250 words) and gracious letter to the editor, using short sentences and paragraphs. Again, stick to one topic and keep the language rational, not emotional. Always sign it, and add your address, phone number and age. Aim at seeing about one letter in ten printed—not a bad batting average!

Alternatively, you can write short articles covering local events in relation to peace. For example, half-nights of prayer and praise for peace, interchurch events, sponsored youth events, local Christian CND meetings, and demonstrations. Demonstrations do give public profile and they can work—they did against slavery, Sunday trading, and for Christian Valeri Barinov's freedom from the USSR. Such copy will often be gladly accepted by the local freebies which rarely employ reporters. Try it and see!

How about news items in local radio? Local hospital radio is often crying out for volunteer help, and often has vacancies for the 'religious' slot.

Do-it-yourself checklist 1

Here's a DIY checklist on what you can do personally, before we look at what the church as a whole can do.

1. Pray, keeping a peace prayer diary.
2. Join a peace organisation, eg Christian CND.
3. Buy a (Christian) peace magazine regularly and get informed.
4. Use peace stickers and slogans.
5. Encourage others through Bible study, prayer triplets, etc.
6. Get involved in school debates, or school projects.
7. Write to your local paper; get on to local or hospital radio.
8. Write to your local MP or visit his clinic.
9. Be a conscientious objector.
10. Refuse to look at military-related jobs as a career.
11. Campaign against war taxes because there'll come a time when you are paying taxes and some of those will support the defence industry.

Giving the church away

We need the Holy Spirit, the bringer of peace (Rom 14:17), in our lives, our families and our churches, if we are to change the world through his power. If we, like Jesus, are to see prisoners released from wrong beliefs about war and peace; if we are to be good news to the poor and oppressed who are the losers in the arms race; if we are to bring healing and wholeness to the physically, emotionally and spiritually sick, then we, like

Jesus, need to be filled with the Holy Spirit. Only the power of God (the Greek word used for power is *dunamis*, giving us the English word 'dynamite') can overcome the power of nuclear bombs. The promise of Zechariah 4:6, made long ago, is still an inspiring one today: ' "Not by might nor by power, but by my Spirit," says the Lord Almighty.'

Prayer begins the process of peace-making through changing individuals, bringing peace within them. That peace must be modelled in our community, that is the church, as well as in our individual lives. As the body of Jesus Christ here on earth, we are a 'trailer' for heaven. We are the only Bible that many people will ever read. Jim Wallis put it like this: 'We have nothing to share with the world other than that which we are sharing with one another.' The Apostle Paul put it: 'There is neither Jew nor Greek, slave nor free, male nor female, for you are all one in Christ Jesus' (Gal 3:28).

So, when you've looked at your own life, look at your church life. Put right any wrong relationships, any enmity, any party spirit. Elders against deacons. PCC against the vicar. Old against young. Charismatic against anti-charismatic. Traditionalism against change. Black against white, male against female, middle class against working class, unemployed against employed! What is important here is not that we sacrifice principles but that we allow the Holy Spirit to adjust attitudes. A church that fights using force in any of these or other areas loses the battle both on earth and in the heavenlies. Paul said that God's 'intent was that now, through the church, the manifold wisdom of God should be made known to the rulers and authorities in the heavenly realms' (Eph 3:10. But if the church is behaving contrary to God's ways and wisdom, then this intent cannot be fulfilled. We also need to look actively at ways in which congregations can relate to other congregations (remember Jesus Christ's prayer for unity in John 17), and to the surrounding community. Look at your church's social action programme for helping the old, the sick and the poor, because that's part of the gospel of peace. Can you introduce world peace as a theme in your family or youth services? Or into the church prayer meeting or Bible study? My own fellowship has a church member (not a leader) who organised a debate on nuclear power which got local press coverage. You could visit other church YPF's and youth services and talk about the theme of peace. It all counts.

Talk with your youth and church leaders about developing a church peace group for prayer and study which can inform the church and initiate action on local issues. Perhaps your church could support Christian people who change their jobs because their employment had involved them in the war-machine issues. Perhaps your church could support military personnel who prayerfully choose to stay in the forces, supporting them with love and care and prayers and not just disagreeing with them. Perhaps you can get your church involved in a school project (or school Christian Union project) on peace, helping with resources like speakers, library resources, videos and films, etc. There's a resource list at the back of this book to help you do just that. Most GCSE RE courses or personal and situational ethics courses have a section dealing with ethical and world issues which includes war and violence. Get involved!

Do-it-yourself checklist number 2

Here's a DIY checklist on what you can do in your church, before we look at the national and international issues and alternatives.

1. Begin to work out any wrong relationships in the church.
2. Be involved in social action.
3. Try to link church to church in peaceful projects that demonstrate unity (John 17), especially celebration and evangelism (which is ultimate peacemaking).
4. Take family or youth services on a peace theme in your own church and in others.
5. Get articles into the church magazine.
6. Get prayer requests (and yourself!) into the church prayer meeting.
7. The issue of war, violence and peace could make a good church or youth fellowship Bible study.
8. They can also make a good church debate, attracting local media.
9. The church can be a support base for those Christians who have left military related jobs out of conviction.
10. And a base for those who, out of conviction, haven't.
11. Links of church to school and college will be a vital resource to train youth in peaceful alternatives.

With all of these points above, remember to consult your leaders, and remember that while the church can decide principles, it's for individuals to apply them through policies. Don't let peace issues cause war in your church!

So far, our alternatives have been personal and church-based. They involve us in looking at our own attitudes and prayer lives as individuals and as members of Jesus Christ's body. What else can we do?

The big wide world

Are there any viable ways forward to ease national and international tensions, and to build a practical defence system without resort to war and violence? We need to be clear that it is right to defend what is good; the question is not do you defend, but how you defend—it's not what we do, but how we do it.

There are a number of practical alternatives. Some have already been tried with some success. Others have remained theory because no one has ever bothered to try them out properly. All depend on personal and church involvement first; we need to be faithful in the small things before we tackle the large (Lk 16:10).

Treaties

Pacts and treaties have been relatively ineffective so far, and some major opportunities squandered through selfishness and fear. Nonetheless, pacts do use the existing international laws and some have worked, not least recent negotiations to reduce the nuclear arsenals and not just slow down their growth. For these we can be thankful. They include such relatively successful treaties as the Partial Test Ban Treaty (1963), The Antarctic Treaty (1959), The Sea Bed Treaty (1971), The Treaty of Tlateloko (1967) (which bans nuclear weapons in twenty-two out of twenty-four Latin American States voluntarily) and The Convention on Biological and Toxic Weapons (1972) Pacts do add legal reasons to the moral and common-sense ones against war. They do clarify the law, and can act as a restraint on governmental changes, as well as models for other governments. They at least head towards a neutral, international arbitration, and pave the way towards war treaties by setting a precedent of dialogue. There are about twelve major treaties in force today. They need our support.

Conferences

Treaties can also be an important part of international conferences, which help in building confidence. The 1975 Helsinki conference established an agreement between nations to give advance warning of military manoeuvres, and to exchange observers of such manoeuvres, both military and scientific, from country to country so that potential enemies could verify that war wasn't being begun secretly. Such exchanges can be encouraged by our prayers, letters and use of local media. We can also lobby our MPs to move on to industrial, technological, commercial, cultural and educational exchanges, and not just military and scientific ones. We need to concentrate on the positive as well as the negative, and view the potential enemy in a more human light.

Verification helps

Multilateral disarmament as a step towards unilateral disarmament is more manageable now than it used to be, which is a good thing. This is because of agreements like the Helsinki conferences on exchange of observers, and because of more accurate verification procedures, which can mean that satellites can pick up details of one foot objects from a distance of one hundred miles, and radars can spot an object the size of a football from a distance of two thousand miles. There are no longer only two choices between either multi or unilateral disarmament. You've probably never heard of transarmament, because nobody's trying it seriously, although there are historical precedents for its working well. Transarmament is where the nations all adopt a different system of non-military defence based mainly on civil non co-operation. More of this a little later.

Economics and common sense

Economics and common sense might prevail in the ending of the arms race; they've got to be on the side of disarmament if only because of rising costs! They have certainly been a major consideration in the USSR's internal adoption of *glasnost* and *perestroika*. Military expenditure frequently outstrips and increases inflation because of the rising prices of components used in jobs that demand a high wage for no visible, usable consumer products. Money spent on arms could be spent on technology for the civilian sector, which is one reason why Japan, with a relatively low military expenditure, has zoomed ahead in the civilian technology race. Military expenditure can raise unemployment levels. If an equal amount of money was spent in other sectors (education, health, building, etc) more jobs would be created. Militry-linked jobs are money eaters, not manpower eaters. And of course the more money spent on arms, the less spent on alms! Less money for the most needy, both in our countries and in the aid given to the Third World. When will economics and common sense prevail to slow down and finally stop this lunatic arms race?

Economics also provides an alternative not properly tried because of vested interest. That's the alternative of effective embargos on trade with nuclear powers. Or embargos on technological exchange with such powers. Or boycotts of imports and produce from countries which break treaty agreements, or disallow verification procedures, or stockpile nuclear or chemical weapons. Governments alone (including the United Kingdom's) are unlikely to pursue these routes fully because of vested interests (for example, our own exports to such countries). But pressure at the local level (prayer, letters, media, petitions, constitutional clinics, demonstrations, etc) *can* change a government's mind. The last few years have seen much evidence that this kind of action is effective. We've seen prisoners released—for example, Valeri Barinov. The March for Jesus in London attracted fifteen thousand then fifty five thousand people. Nationwide it attracted hundreds of thousands of Christians on to the streets in positive peaceful demonstration of a God who cares, and who expresses that care through his people. It was not a demonstration against something, nor a protest march, but a peaceful, caring, praising and praying mass demonstration of God's desire to forgive, save, heal, restore and bless. We could do with demonstrations like this for world peace, looking to dismantle systems of war and change men's hearts. Peaceful picketing is the next (and I think acceptable) step along from this. And it can start small—in your town or city.

National non-military defence?

The last national/international alternative I want to look at is the one I've already alluded to and the one which we're furthest from. But it's one we could aim at in prayers and in action. Transarmament, described by Ronald Sider and Richard Taylor in their book *Nuclear Holocaust and Christian Hope* (Hodder and Stoughton: London, 1983), is a policy that opens up new thinking and exciting possibilities because it gets away from

what is often a stalemate between the deterrence/multi/
unilateral positions.

It is not so far-fetched as to be unworkable—there
are already precedents in history where this alternative
has had a degree of limited success. The idea is based
on the natural principle that you fight least destruc-
tively with water, not fire. That darkness is overcome
with light, not with more darkness. That love overcomes hate. That peace overcomes violence. From the
Christian's point of view, we can add that it is based on
the principle that it is valid to defend what is good (Isa
1:17), but only and always by putting God and his ways
first and not to defend at any cost, either to you or your
'enemy'. It's based on the fact that any government
(your own or one imposed by a conqueror) must have a
degree of consensus from the people in order to govern.
It can attempt to extract that consensus by costly and
painful violence, but it must have that consensus.
Therefore it can be defeated by positive, active, non-
violent resistance through non-cooperation by the civilian population. And what is more, this has been done!

A little history

In its first three centuries, the early church not only
survived, but grew by resisting cruel Roman rule and
oppression by positive, active, non-violent non-co-operation. But could this work in the face of modern
methods of control and warfare? It did in 1859–67
when Hungary sought to invade and suppress Austria,
and eventually had to pull back defeated. The same
thing happened in 1923 when Germany resisted France
and Belgium without military campaigns. It even
worked during the Second World War between 1940
and 1945 when Germany invaded Norway and waged

internal war against teachers and the church which it saw as two prime agencies it had to destroy in order to maintain its rule over Norway. Because of positive, active, non-violent non-co-operation by the populace (violent opposition would have been easily squashed), Germany failed throughout the war to subdue either the religious or the educational freedom of invaded Norway. When Denmark refused to co-operate with Hitler's dictates to hand over the Jews, 93% of the Jews survived and escaped. The same story happened in Finland, where only 4 out of 2,000 Jews went to concentration camps! Holland was less successful in her attempt to save the Jews, but many escaped—read Corrie Ten Boom's story in *The Hiding Place* (Hodder and Stoughton: London, 1976) Seventy five per cent of French Jews were saved, and 80% of Italian Jews. Bulgaria kept all her Jews safe. I can't help wondering what the results would have been if the same determination went into non-violent resistance to the actual invading army and conquering government as went into saving the Jews?

These are not isolated incidents. Ghandi saw a whole sub-continent freed from very oppressive British rule in 1947 with a plan of non-violent, non-cooperation. Ghana did the same between 1949–57. El Salvador, now often home to bloody military coups, overcame a dictator in 1944 by non-military peaceful means of media coverage, meetings, resignations of key positions, such as doctors, lawyers, teachers and engineers, and by mobilising her people (not the army) against a corrupt government and its dictator. Non-violent general strikes have similarly removed at least seven such dictators in Latin America since then. In the 1950s, Martin Luther King began his peaceful struggle to see black Americans freed from oppression in the USA. Non-violent non-co-operation has worked nationally, both internally and externally, and it can work again. But how?

The ingredients of non-military national defence

1. It needs activity not passivity. Everyone must be mobilised, or such a massive majority as to render those who 'cop out' ineffective.

2. It needs a determination to resist, not a willingness to go along with orders. This will mean a willingness to do what is forbidden (civil disobedience) while remaining subject to the authorities (see Chapter 8).

3. It is non-cooperative, which means you not only do the forbidden, but you refuse to do the bidden!

4. It requires great courage and is costly. People will die. You cannot have a defence system whereby in the event of invasion, no one dies. But not as many will die as if you used military force or nuclear bombs! And it is in keeping with God's heart (do check out Jn 15:20; Mt 10:16–39; 24:9; 5:10; Lk 21:12–19).

5. It creates not an underground resistance or army, but a high-profile people's 'army' of peaceful non-cooperators, civilian based and therefore huge in numbers.

6. It aims to reduce violence in the violent aggressor by meeting it with non-violence, showing up the aggressor for what he is. Christians should be in the forefront of this kind of action (Rom 12:14–21).

7. It sees occupation not as an end to the campaign but instead as a beginning. The war is won by making the territory which has been taken ungovernable, not by

making that territory unreachable, or even worse, in the case of nuclear bombs, uninhabitable.

A scenario

So if the United Kingdom was invaded, what could we do? If the UK had been trained in civilian-based trans-armament defence (using part of the money presently poured into nuclear weapons) we would be able to call a general strike. We would communicate at all times with the invading enemy. We would 'police' our own protestors (as happened in El Salvador in 1944) to ensure peaceful means of protest. There would be general non-co-operation, refusing sales of food, equipment, fuel, water, sanitation, heat and light, except where clear injury—including to the invading enemy—was the outcome. As arrests were made (and torture and killing went on) there would be a strategy to replace those key figures arrested with new ones (as happened with the teachers in Norway in the Second World War). As far as possible, life would be carried out as though no invasion had taken place. We would refuse to pay all taxes. New governments structures would be ignored. No transport or housing would be given to the enemy, no post delivered, and no curfews accepted. Kindness to the enemy in all of this would result in massive troop demoralisation, which is a price too high for any invading army to pay, and would mean we'd have to resist propaganda against the enemy from ourselves, and against ourselves from the enemy.

Make-your-mind-up-time

Such a positive, active, non-violent, non-co-operative, civilian-based response on a *national* scale *could* work. It was George Bernard Shaw who said, 'You see things as they are and ask "why?" but I dream things that never were, and ask "why not?" ' It is feasible. It is an alternative. Of course, it might not work. But then, nuclear deterrence might not work—might destroy us all, and probably would. Which risk would you rather take? Which is the higher cost? There isn't a defence system which is 100% certain. I know which I'd rather try. I know which I'd rather risk. I know which I believe God sanctions. And which he forbids. How about you?

Last Words

I'd like to leave you with a quotation from Ronald Sider and Richard Taylor's book *Nuclear Holocaust and Christian Hope* which I wholeheartedly recommend. Sider quotes Daniel Berrigan, an American writer, on the subject of war, violence and peace.

> We have assumed the name of peacemakers, but we have been, by and large, unwilling to pay any significant price. And because we want the peace with half a heart and half a life and will, the war, of course, continues, because the waging of war by its nature, is total—but the waging of peace, by our own cowardice, is partial. So a whole will and a whole heart and a whole national life bent toward war prevail over these (mere desire for) peace. In every national war we have taken for granted that war shall exact the most rigorous cost, and that the cost shall be paid with cheerful heart. We take it for granted that in wartime families will be separated for long periods, that men will be imprisoned, wounded, driven insane, killed on foreign shores. In favour of such wars, we declare a moratorium on every normal human hope—for marriage, for community, for friendship, for moral conduct towards strangers and the innocent. We are instructed that

depravation and discipline, private grief and public obedience are to be our lot. And we obey. And we bear with it—because bear we must—because war is war, and good war or bad, we are stuck with it and its cost.

But what of the price of peace? I think of the good, decent, peace-loving people I have known by the thousands, and I wonder. How many of them are so afflicted with the wasted disease of normalcy that, even as they declare for peace, their hands reach out with an instinctive spasm in the direction of their loved ones, in the direction of their comforts, their home, their security, their income, their future, their plans—that five year plan of studies, that ten year plan of professional status, that twenty year plan of family growth and unity, that fifty year plan of decent life and honourable natural demise. 'Of course, let us have the peace' we cry, 'But at the same time let us have normalcy, let us lose nothing, let our lives stand intact, let us know neither prison or ill repute nor disruption of ties.' And because we must encompass this and protect that, and because at all costs—at all costs—our hopes must march on schedule, and because it is unheard of that in the name of peace a sword should fall, disjoining that fine and cunning web that our lives have woven, because it is unheard of that good men should suffer injustice or families be sundered our good repute be lost—because of this we cry peace and cry peace, and there is no peace. There is no peace because the making of peace is at least as costly as the making of war—at least as exigent, at least as disruptive, at least as liable to bring disgrace and prison and death in its wake.

There it is. A huge issue practically. A huge issue theologically. A huge price to be paid. I've tried to make it accessible. To find ways to grapple honestly with the arguments and problems. At the end of the day, though, it's not about winning arguments and losing friends, or who argues the best, or quotes the most statistics, or the most Bible references. That's not peace. It's about letting the God of all peace rule in our hearts, to change us one by one into the likeness of his dear Son, Jesus, the Prince of peace.

I hope this book not only stimulates your mind into thinking, but also your spirit into submission and devotion to Christ and your body into action! It's not just about information, though that's important (Hos 4:6). It's also about vision (Prov 29:18) so that together information and vision might produce transformation—because that is our spiritual worship:

> Therefore, I urge you, brothers, in view of God's mercy, to offer your bodies as living sacrifices, holy and pleasing to God—this is your spiritual worship act of. Do not conform any longer to the pattern of this world, but be transformed by the renewing of your mind. Then you will be able to test and approve what God's will is—his good, pleasing and perfect will (Rom 12:1–2).

Recommended Books

Evangelical Peacemakers, *Decide for Peace* (Marshall, Morgan and Scott: Basingstoke, 1986).

John Gladwin, ed, *Dropping the Bomb* (Hodder and Stoughton: London, 1985).

Kenneth Greet, *The Big Sin* (Marshall, Morgan and Scott: Basingstoke, 1982).

David Sheppard, *Bias to the Poor* (Hodder and Stoughton: London, 1978).

Ronald Sider, *Christ and Violence* (Lion: Tring, 1979).

Ronald Sider and Kenneth Taylor, *Nuclear Holocaust and Christian Hope* (Hodder and Stoughton: London, 1983).

Ronald Sider, *Rich Christians in an Age of Hunger* (Hodder and Stoughton: London, 1978).

Tom Sine, *The Mustard Seed Conspiracy* (MARC Europe: Bromley, 1985).

John Stott, *Issues Facing Christians Today* (Marshall, Morgan and Scott: Basingstoke, 1986).

Recommended Resources

Christian Organisations

Anglican Pacifist Fellowship
St Mary's Church House
Bayswater Road
Oxford
OX3 9EY

Christian CND
11 Goodwin Street
London
N4 3HQ

Christian Movement for Peace
Stowford House
Bayswater Road
Oxford
OX3 9SA

Commission for International Justice and Peace
(Roman Catholic)
38 Ecclestone Square
London
SW1

Pax Christi (Roman Catholic)
Pottery Lane
St Francis of Assisi Centre
London
W11 4NQ

Non-Christian Organisations

Armaments and Disarmament Information Unit
Mantell Building
University of Sussex
Falmer
East Sussex

Arms Control and Disarmament Research Unit
Foreign and Commonwealth Office
London

Peace Tax Campaign
36 Thurlow Road
Leicester
LE2 1YE

War Resisters International
55 Dawes Street
London
SE17 1EL

World Disarmament Campaign
Churches' Liaison—The Rev Will Elliott
35 Station Road
Harpenden
Herts

Audio visual aids

Hiroshima-Nagasaki August 1945, 15 minutes 16mm
film, Concord Films Council, 201 Felixtowe Road,
Ipswich, Suffolk IP3 9BJ.
The War Game, 49 minutes 16mm film, Concord Films
Council, 201 Felixtowe Road, Ipswich, Suffolk IP3
9BJ.
War Without Winners, 27 minutes 16mm film, Concord
Films Council, 201 Felixtowe Road, Ipswich, Suffolk
IP3 9BJ.
War To End All Wars, 22 minutes slide or film strip,
Concord Films Council, 201 Felixtowe Road,
Ipswich, Suffolk IP3 9BJ.

Resource packs for church use

Christian CND Resource Pack, 11 Goodwin Street,
London N4 3HQ.
Christians At The Crossroads, 11 Goodwin Street,
London N4 3HQ.
Peacemaking In A Nuclear Age, Scottish Episcopal
Church, Bishops House, Fairmont Road, Perth,
Scotland PH2 7AP.